AND

MAN
CREATED
GOD

For Linda

AND
MAN
CREATED
GOD

Is God a Human Invention?

Robert Banks

LION

A Lion Book
an imprint of
Lion Hudson plc
Wilkinson House, Jordan Hill Road,
Oxford OX2 8DR, England
www.lionhudson.com
ISBN 978 0 7459 5543 8

First edition 2011
10 9 8 7 6 5 4 3 2 1 0

Acknowlegments

Scripture quotation on page 10 taken from the Holy Bible, New International
Version, copyright © 1973, 1978, 1984 International Bible Society. Used by
permission of Hodder & Stoughton, a member of the Hodder Headline Group.
All rights reserved. 'NIV' is a trademark of International Bible Society. UK
trademark number 1448790.

Distributed by:
UK: Marston Book Services, PO Box 269, Abingdon, Oxon, OX14 4YN
USA: Trafalgar Square Publishing, 814 N. Franklin Street, Chicago, IL 60610
USA Christian Market: Kregel Publications, PO Box 2607, Grand Rapids,
Michigan 49501

This book has been printed on paper and board independently certified as
having been produced from sustainable forests.

A catalogue record for this book is available
from the British Library

Typeset in 10.5/14 Latin 725 BT
Printed in Great Britain by Clays Ltd, St Ives plc

Contents

Acknowledgments

My thanks to John Kleinig who, many years ago, read my initial attempt at discussing this topic and suggested I think about a different way of presenting it. Also to Pat Marshall who, after I decided to shelve the project for a time, every so often asked me when I was going to take it up again. When I had completed a new version of the book, John Drane helpfully opened up a connection with Lion Hudson that led to their accepting it for publication.

I appreciated the opportunity provided by teaching a graduate course on apologetics at Fuller Theological Seminary, Pasadena, to share a chapter of the book. Also the invitation to give a seminar outlining one of its main themes at the Centre for the Study of Christian Thought and Experience at Macquarie University, Sydney.

Thanks to the editors of several journals, including *Religion*, *The Journal of Religion*, and the *Evangelical Quarterly*, for being able to draw on material originally contained in them, as well as to InterVarsity Press for the chance to look at the book *Idols* by Julian Hardyman in advance of its publication.

I'm grateful to my editors, Kate Kirkpatrick, Miranda Lever, and David Moloney, whose insightful comments have helped me produce a more concise, focused and accessible work. And my most heartfelt thanks go to my wife, Linda, for continually encouraging me as I was writing the book but most of all for opening up a new chapter, indeed new volume, in my life overall.

Robert Banks
Sydney, August 2010

FOREWORD

I first became interested in the question raised by this book – whether God created us or we created God – many years ago. This happened at quite a personal level, not just an academic one. I grew up in a family that did not engage in religious practices or even talk about God. Though I had had some contact with the church in my primary years, it was not until my mid-teens that I began to seriously wonder about how belief in God arose. However, I began to experience doubts while studying philosophy at university, and though I returned to a position of faith a couple of years later, these doubts occasionally resurfaced.

Then I began to come across writers who approached the question of God from a different angle to the ones I was accustomed to. Instead of seeking to disprove the existence of God, they were more interested in asking what it was that motivated people to imagine such a being in the first place. For a time this put a cloud over my religious commitments. I went through a period of considerable doubt, confusion and, for a short time, unbelief. How could I confidently discern when and whether I was really relating to a God who had my best interests at heart or was just projecting my own interests onto an imaginary person? I did not know anyone I could talk to who had experienced, or was going through, the same struggle. I did not know, and for a while could not find, any books that addressed the issue in a substantial way. It was only over a period of time that I began to discover a way through the thicket of thorny questions that kept pressing in on me, and finally regain the full confidence of faith that I had first experienced in my mid-teens.

This process involved more than finding satisfactory arguments on which to ground my belief, as these can never approach the certainty of scientific or mathematical propositions. It involved the discovery that the vision of life proposed by these critics was not expansive enough to cover all that made up reality, and that what it required of me was not radical enough to be sufficiently persuasive.

When, some years later, I was able to explore issues of atheism and belief while working in a research institute, I gladly took up the opportunity. I decided to focus on the views of some of the leading modern critics of religion, especially on their ideas about how belief in God arose. Could belief in God be traced, as the main monotheistic religions believed, to divine revelation or was it invented by human imagination? Was it true, as the first chapter of the Bible states, that "God created man in his own image" (Genesis 1:26), or was it the case that "Man created God in his"? If I had not experienced religious doubts before, my interest in this topic would have been purely intellectual. My previous struggles over these issues meant that investigating the topic was as much a matter of the heart as it was the head. Aspects of this research were subsequently published as articles in several journals of religion.

A little later I decided to attempt something more extensive. But after completing a book-length draft covering half the material, I stopped. This was partly because I felt it was not the kind of book I wanted to write. It was also partly because the times were changing. In the wider culture, interest was moving away from discussion of atheism and religion in favour of new forms of spirituality. Eastern religions and New Age philosophies were replacing atheism and agnosticism as the main alternatives to traditional religions.

This has now changed with the emergence of the so-called "New Atheism" in the public arena. Though some of this is not particularly new at all, it has evoked considerable interest and attracted a wide readership. A growing number of books have appeared from authors like Daniel Dennett, Richard Dawkins, Sam Harris, Christopher Hitchens, and Michael Onfray. Their views have also been taken up on radio, television, the internet, and on the conference circuit. While responses to their efforts vary – even from those who share their general outlook – they have clearly touched a cultural nerve that so far shows no sign of diminishing. The question of whether we created God or God created us may only be a small part of their discussion, but it also appears in other writings and settings.

In response, I have sought to approach the issue in an accessible yet thoughtful way, and in a form that gives attention to experiential as well as intellectual factors. This involves telling the story of how the critique arose, developed, and became increasingly influential. It has its origin in a most unexpected place, passes through some interesting mutations, and undergoes a complete turnaround at the hands of its leading modern interpreters. To preserve some of the personal character of the key contributors, I have included frequent quotations from their writings. The central part of the book evaluates the leading modern approaches to the critique as honestly and sympathetically as possible. This focuses on its most innovative and influential advocates, as well as a selection of key figures influenced by them. In addition to questioning where I think they are wrong, unclear, or confused, I seek to acknowledge where I think they are right and at one level continue to pose a challenge to believers.

It is not enough, as some do, to simply agree with these critics, for the simple reason that they do not always agree among themselves. A number of logical, historical, and empirical questions can also be raised against their views. Nor is not enough, as others do, to simply dismiss these critics because they do not believe in God or argue that he is a purely human invention. For even if their views on this are not fully persuasive, it is hard to deny the force of their criticisms against some ideas of God. Whether what I have written does justice to the topic, and to the experience of those who have wrestled with it in the past and still do today, I leave it to the reader to decide. I have done the best I can and will be interested to see how others respond.

Finally, where I have used the word "Man" it is human beings in general that is meant – as in the title of this book, which inverts one of the opening statements of the Bible. Similarly where – mostly in quotations, including those from critics of religion – the pronoun "he" is used for "God", this is not meant to imply anything about God's gender. Further reflection on this can be found in my book on *God as Worker: Journeys into the Mind, Heart and Imagination of God*, in which I consider the way God is portrayed through both feminine and masculine images but ultimately in a way which transcends both.

PART ONE

BACK ON THE PUBLIC AGENDA

1

The Renewal of an Old
Attack on Religion

A new development is taking place in the wider culture. Those who query or reject religion are becoming more vocal in their stance against it. Weary of Christians publicly advertising their faith, a group of atheists in London in 2008 created bus posters declaring, "There's probably no God. Now stop worrying and enjoy your life." When a similar group in Chicago started up a public transport campaign, they went further and for their slogan chose: "In the beginning, man created God." According to the group's spokesman, the slogan "espouses the idea that man created God as well as all religions", and "encourages public and critical examination of the merits of religious belief".

Most recently, just before Christmas 2010, the American Atheists society commissioned a billboard to be placed on a major road leading into New York City. Above a picture of the three wise men following a star across the desert were the words "You know it's a myth".

This viewpoint is additionally being expressed in other popular ways. One internet expression of this is the appearance of advertisements for a variety of T-shirts bearing the logo "Man created God". On websites such as Facebook and YouTube, the same message appears in the form of music videos and graphic designs. There are also blogs and forums devoted to a discussion of the topic.

Interest in the subject has resulted in the production of self-published books dealing directly with the issue. An example of this is D. G. McLeod's *Then Man Created God: The Truth about Believing a Lie* (2009), which is an aggressive attack on all forms of religious belief and practice. From a different field altogether, there is the novel by Steve Toltz, *A Fraction of the Whole*, which was shortlisted for the Man Booker prize. Much of this is cast in the form of down-to-earth monologues or conversations around a wide range of topics. These focus on basic human concerns, including whether or not there is a God and how ideas of God came into being. As the chief protagonist at one point in the novel remarks: "To me, it was obvious man created God in his own image. Man hasn't the imagination to come up with a God totally unlike him."[1]

Why do we do this? We find it hard to believe that the being that most inspires imagination, creativity, and empathy, could be one of us. Recent films reflecting on everyday events and their consequences, such as *Winged Creatures,* also raise questions about what motivates belief in God. Within this, the story explores how vulnerable we are to fashioning or influencing our conceptions of God according to our own needs and desires.

So, then, in various ways the possibility that God is partly or wholly a man-made affair has come back on the public agenda. In other respects, however, preliminary forms of the question have always been at hand. A prime example occurs when some parents and religious instructors seek to encourage a religious attitude in their children. When told that God made the universe, most children simply accept what they hear. But after a time, generally between the ages of six and nine, some unexpectedly ask: "If God made everything, then who made God?" This is a good place to begin our investigation.

Who made God?

This question shows that a child is beginning to wonder about one of the big questions of life. In asking it they are not really querying whether God exists. They are simply trying to work out how similar or different God is to everything else in their world – particularly those who are older than them. Since these are the only categories they have for understanding God, it's a perfectly natural question. The answer a child usually gets runs something like this: "God is not the same as us. He wasn't made by anyone else. He has just always been there."

For most children such an answer is enough – for the time being. It satisfies their curiosity about God. But occasionally they will want to take the question a stage further. Phillip Adams, a popular Australian journalist and broadcaster, is one example. His father was a minister and his mother was also a devout Christian. One day he asked them: "If everything began from something else, then who began God?" On hearing the conventional answer to his question, he decided that such a being was highly unlikely. This was the start of his journey into atheism.

As the children of believing parents grow up, they learn that the answer given to their question echoed the opening words in the Bible. After God created heaven and earth, states Genesis, he "created Man in his own image". As a child's understanding of God develops, especially if it is more than a second-hand belief, many come to the conclusion that their original question was inadequate. Others, for various reasons, might begin to doubt whether they can ever know for certain if God exists, or simply give up belief in God altogether, dismissing it as a childish fantasy.

In some cases the question "Who made God?" then comes back on the scene in a new form. An example of this thought process is evident in the physicist Stephen Hawking's best-selling book on time. In it, he reflects on what it was that started the universe. "Does it need a creator", he asks, "and if so … who created him?"[2] So complex are the issues involved, Hawking concludes, that the question has no credible answer. In this matter we have no alternative but to live on the far edge of uncertainty, indeed improbability.

Other scientists add to this discussion by raising the question of whether humanity, specifically its brain, created God, arguing that the way people are neurologically wired may determine whether they believe in such a being or not.[3]

Several of the so-called "New Atheists" are more definite. According to the biologist Richard Dawkins, the beauty and intricacy of the universe make it quite understandable that people should wonder if it comes from the work of a "Grand Designer". But since such a creator would have to be at least as complex as the universe itself, the problem is only pushed further back. It automatically raises the question "Who, or What, created God?"[4] The cultural critic Sam Harris regards God as fiction and agrees that attempts to prove his existence cannot answer why the causal chain has to stop with God. Why shouldn't it just go on for ever?[5] For the scientist Daniel Dennett, God is a childish myth that has become an adult delusion, rather like Santa Claus.[6] This makes the query "Who made God?" less an exploratory question about God's nature and more a basic premise of his impossibility.

I will assess these claims later. Instead we first turn to those who take this approach a step further. What for the most part is only mentioned in passing by the thinkers mentioned above is explored in a more overt way by other figures.

Who made God up?

Many who become agnostics or atheists are content to simply raise objections to traditional views of God and to provide arguments for a more humanist approach to life. For the most part, the writers mentioned above all regard human understanding and experience alone as the source of values and goals to live by. If occasionally these writers ask how belief in God arises in the first place, they do not explore this in any significant way. For example, though Richard Dawkins identifies "wish fulfilment" – what we would like rather than what is actually the case – as a basic feature of all religious systems, he does not explore this any further. Why should the wish that God be there take the particular forms that it does? How could so many people down through the centuries come to believe in someone who does not exist? While many have accepted the existence of imaginary beings like fairies, ghosts, and vampires, the majority generally quietly and gradually outgrow such beliefs.

One of the New Atheists who raises this issue briefly is André Comte Sponville. He asks what it is that people wish for more than anything else. Leaving aside our baser desires, he says what we wish for most is:

> ... *first, not to die, not completely, not irreversibly;*
> *second, to be united with the loved ones we have lost;*
> *third, for justice and peace to triumph; finally, and*

> *most important, to be loved. Now, what does religion*
> *tell us – and the Christian religion in particular?*
> *That we shall not die, or not really; that we shall*
> *rise from the dead and thus be reunited with the*
> *loved ones we have lost; that justice and peace will*
> *prevail in the end; and, finally, that we are already*
> *the object of infinite love. Who could ask for more?*
> *No one, of course! This is what makes religion so*
> *very suspicious, it is too good to be true!...*[7]

But it is precisely the thought that Christianity's ideas are too good to be true, he says, that makes it improbable and gives us every reason to suspect it springs from our own wishes.

Taking the next step, Christopher Hitchens suggests in passing that "God did not create man in his own image. Evidently it was the other way round... ".[8] But in his treatment he only gives this brief attention. More substantially Michael Onfray links this with earlier philosophical critiques of religion, arguing that God is a fictional product of our projections:

> *Man creates God in their own inverted image.*
> *Mortal, finite, limited, suffering from all these*
> *constraints, haunted by the desire for completeness,*
> *human beings invent a power endowed with*
> *precisely the opposite characteristics ... at whose feet*
> *they kneel and finally prostrate themselves. I am*
> *mortal, but God is immortal. I am finite, but God*
> *is infinite. I am limited, but God knows no limits.*
> *I do not know everything, but God is omniscient.*
> *I cannot do everything, but God is omnipotent. I*
> *am not blessed with the gift of ubiquity, but God is*

> *omnipresent. I was created, but God is uncreated. I*
> *am weak, but God is the Almighty. I am on earth,*
> *but God is in heaven. I am imperfect, but God is*
> *perfect. I am nothing, but God is everything, and*
> *so on. Religion thus … proposes the creation of an*
> *imaginary world falsely invested with truth.*[9]

The first writer I came across who advocated this view was one who helped put it on the public agenda in a previous generation. As a young man, Bertrand Russell (1872–1970) was quite interested in discussions about the origin of the universe. Initially he accepted the idea that there had to be an original cause of everything that exists, behind which it was impossible to go. Then:

> *… one day, at the age of eighteen, I read John*
> *Stuart Mill's* Autobiography, *and I there found*
> *this sentence: "My father taught me that the*
> *question, Who made me? cannot be answered, since*
> *it immediately suggests the further question, Who*
> *made God?" That very simple sentence showed me,*
> *as I still think, the fallacy in the argument of the*
> *First Cause … It is exactly of the same nature as*
> *the Indian's view, that the world rested upon an*
> *elephant and the elephant rested upon a tortoise;*
> *and when they said, "How about the tortoise?"*
> *the Indian said, "Suppose we change the subject"*
> *… The idea that things must have a beginning is*
> *really due to the poverty of our imagination.*[10]

How then did belief in God come into existence? According to Russell, religion is mainly based upon fear. Negatively it arose from our terror of the unknown and positively from our desire to have a cosmic elder brother to help us in our troubles. The earliest gods created by our primitive ancestors were primarily characterized by power. Later, as their moral awareness grew, our ancestors preferred gods who reflected higher ideals. Instead of it being the case that "God created man in his own image", on the contrary "*Man* created God in *his* own image"! We are not personal because he is personal and has imprinted us with something of his nature. Rather we conceive him as personal because we imagine him to be something like us and have imprinted on him something of our own higher nature.

According to Russell this took place slowly over a long period of time. The gods pictured by the Greeks and Romans were a halfway house in this development. While they embodied some higher ideals, they also demonstrated some typical human flaws. In some ways they were similar to humans but operated on a larger scale. For Russell, the genius of the Jewish and Christian view was that it replaced the idea of a pantheon of deities with belief in one superior, universal God, characterized by love as well as power. This view influenced other religions such as Islam and continues to resound today in the universal claims of various ideologies.[11]

The downside of this all-embracing, perfect, and powerful "make-believe" divinity, argues Russell, is that it becomes an even more seductive crutch on which we can lean. We displace our yearnings, hopes, and goals onto him and look to him to overcome our uncertainties, challenges, and limitations. God becomes a kind of cosmic "Superman" through whom we hope to aspire to our potential and deal with our failures. This is illusory, for ultimately he prevents us making real progress in both areas. Only when we draw upon the strength that comes from within us and each other, and are willing to grow up and take responsibility for our individual and corporate lives, can this take place.[12]

We find a similar view reappearing today, with some new features, in the cultural anthropologist Stewart Elliott Guthrie's picturesquely entitled work *Faces in the Clouds*. He builds his approach to religion on humanity's need for a certain kind of understanding rather than for a certain kind of experience or meaning. With this he notes that a common feature of all religions is "communication with humanlike, yet nonhuman, beings through some form of symbolic action ... Humanlike models persist because they identify and account for the crucial component of the world: humans and their activities and effects."[13]

This means that anthropomorphic ways of describing and talking about the gods – describing their character and activities in terms drawn from human experience – is quite plausible and reasonable, even if on reflection it is mistaken.

Who made God over?

Even though a majority of people today grow up with little exposure to religion, most still develop some idea of God. This happens whether their attitude towards God is negative, positive, or just indifferent. As a result, when such people use the word "God" they often understand it in different, sometimes contradictory, ways. This is not only between adherents of different religions but even within the same one. Think of disagreements between Catholics and Protestants, not only in their doctrines and practices but also in some respects their views of God. While both believe that God is loving and holy, merciful and righteous, forgiving and wrathful, the emphasis they place on these, the immediacy of their relationship to God, and the way these work out in people's lives, varies. Sometimes members of both traditions suggest that some of these differences derive from the intrusion of human ideas into understanding the divine.

Consider the difference between what is described as progressive and traditional Christian views of God. Adherents of the former view argue that traditional depictions of God are more fixated on his holiness and justice than on his love and mercy. This is due, they believe, to the legacy of ancient and medieval elements in Christianity that our modern understanding and sensibilities feel to be inadequate. The idea that God required satisfaction for offences committed against him sprang from less humane ideas than are acceptable today. It should be replaced by a stronger emphasis on his unconditional love and forgiveness.

Or consider the difference between more mystically and rationally theologically oriented believers. The former reject a too rigidly defined view of God in favour of a more intimately experiential or transcendent one. The ex-nun Karen Armstrong, author of the best-selling book *A History of God*, is a representative of this view. The Jewish God, who began as one of several deities worshipped by the Israelites, was originally a savage, partisan god of war. It was only as a result of some profound national experiences that he evolved into the unique, almighty transcendent being proclaimed by the prophets. This God met the new psychological needs of the people of Israel and in this the Jewish faith was no different from any other. Indeed Armstrong goes as far as to say that "when they attributed their own human feelings and experiences to Yahweh, the prophets were in an important sense creating God in their own image ... As long as this projection does not become an end in itself, it can be useful and beneficial."[14]

To avoid becoming obsolete, Armstrong says, all religions change and develop, and each generation has to create its image of God. For her, the strength of this personal idea of God, as of subsequent Christian and Islamic developments, is the way it establishes the dignity of the individual and also a more humane society. Its weakness is that it can too easily become an idolatrous projection of humanity's hopes and fears. We are prone to picture God in terms that are too purely personal at the expense of his cosmic character. It is only a more contemplative approach to the divine that can escape this dilemma, and it is no accident that this developed in all three monotheistic religions, as the Jewish Kabbalah, Christian Mystics, and Sufi movement within Islam testify.

Ordinary believers are also likely to add to or take away from whatever understanding of God they inherit from their upbringing, denomination, politics, or even gender. All are susceptible to adding something of their individual impressions or understanding of God to these. All are vulnerable to viewing God in ways they would prefer him to be like. They might do this because they would like God to respond to particular hopes they have, benefits they desire, or consequences they want to avoid.

A good example of this comes from the early life of the well-known author C. S. Lewis (1898–1963). In his autobiography he talks about the role of religion in his upbringing and recalls his reaction to the unexpected death of his mother. Although he was not brought up in a vitally religious way, he was taught to dutifully say his prayers and attend church. But in his ninth year his mother was diagnosed with cancer.

> *When her case was pronounced hopeless I remembered what I had been taught; that prayers*

offered in faith would be granted. I accordingly set myself to produce by willpower a firm belief that my prayers for her recovery would be successful; and, as I thought, I achieved it. When nevertheless she died I shifted my ground and worked myself into a belief that there would be a miracle. The interesting thing is that my disappointment produced no results beyond itself ... I think the belief into which I had hypnotised myself was itself too irreligious for its failure to cause any religious revolution. I had approached God, or my idea of God, without love, without awe, even without fear. He was, in my mental picture of this miracle, to appear neither as Saviour nor as Judge, but merely as a magician ... It never crossed my mind that the tremendous contact I had solicited should have any consequences beyond restoring the status quo. I imagine that a "faith" of this kind is often generated in children.[15]

Interestingly, our tendency to foist our own ideas onto God now appears to have scientific support. An Australian–American survey entitled "Creating God in One's Own Image", recently published in the *Proceedings of the National Academy of Sciences*, sought to discover how believers determine the will of God on important topics. Using surveys, psychological manipulation, and brain imaging, they conducted seven studies. Four of these surveyed participants' views on such controversial issues as abortion and the death penalty. They were also asked about what some famous people and God himself believed. The psychologists then altered participants' views slightly with various techniques, such as writing and delivering a speech on a topic from a particular viewpoint in front of a video camera. The final study involved taking brain images of believers as they thought about their own beliefs versus those of God or another person. The team found that many of the same brain regions became active when people thought about their own views and God's views, but that different areas lit up when contemplating the views of other people.

From their research the team concluded that people subconsciously projected their own attitudes to controversial issues onto God. When their views changed slightly, they thought that God's views had shifted too. Thus: "Manipulating people's own beliefs affected their estimates of God's beliefs more than it affected estimates of other people's beliefs."[16]

Though participants believed that God wanted them to act as if they were a kind of living moral compass, unlike an actual compass inferences about God's beliefs may instead have pointed people further in whatever direction they were already facing. However, although people's perceptions of God's attitudes on an issue could be "nudged" slightly, there did seem to be limits as to how radically people would change their views.

Is there any way out of our tendency to impose, however unconsciously, our all-too-human ideas onto our view of God? The main answer given to this is that human beings should acknowledge the need for God to reveal himself to them rather than develop their own understanding of God. I shall return to the merits of this answer later but here it must be acknowledged that it does not *absolutely* escape the problem. The simple reason for this is that those who take their stand based on the Scripture do not all agree on what it says about God's nature and activity. Those who take the Bible seriously can still differ on the scope of God's grace, the role of God's influence on human freewill, and how to view God's power in everyday affairs. In other words, their images of God differ. So, by itself, an appeal to divine authority of this kind does not answer all the questions.

* . * . *

The upshot of all this is that the question of whether God created us or whether we created God, does not equate with a neat division between those who acknowledge God and those who do not. Both, whether as a basis for unbelief or one of faith, are vulnerable to picturing God in human terms. The issue remains one that both have to grapple with. In order to work out how much human beings have played a part in inventing and portraying God, the best way forward is initially to look backwards. When did the view that humankind created God arise? Who first thought of it? Where did this take place? Why did it surface? What was its impact? As we will see, answering these questions leads us to some interesting, and ultimately surprising, discoveries.

PART TWO

EARLY ADVOCATES OF A SCEPTICAL VIEW

2

A New Challenge to the Gods

The idea that we invented God rather than God inventing us is often regarded as a modern one. While it only came to full expression in the last two centuries, its roots actually lie almost three millennia back. Those who are aware of its earlier origins generally trace it back to several ancient Greek thinkers in the sixth century BC. For a time this is what I thought myself, but closer investigation pointed to another group altogether – one whose identity comes as something of a surprise.

The first to broach the idea of human beings having created gods were a number of Old Testament Jewish prophets from the eighth century BC onwards. Why has their role here been overlooked? Perhaps it is because it was assumed that a serious critique of religion could only arise from outside a religious perspective. However, some of the most fundamental challenges to religion down through the centuries have come from radical believers who criticized its distortion and co-option from within.

The first Jewish critics

Israel's religion differed from that of its neighbours in its commitment to one God. Although there was a short-lived experiment with the sole worship of the sun god Amun-Re in fourteenth-century BC Egypt, it was only in Israel that a fully fledged monotheistic belief took hold. While at the popular level some did not always hold to this, from the time of Moses (around the twelfth century BC onwards) monotheism became the official belief.

The few references in the Old Testament that seem to acknowledge the reality of other gods, such as the Canaanite deity Baal, mainly recognize the existence of foreign religions or mention them in an ironical or rhetorical way. What begins to surface in the writings of eighth-century BC prophets – such as Amos, Micah, Nahum, and Isaiah – is the claim that these gods were manufactured by human creators. Humankind physically makes representations of the gods and then regards what is actually lifeless and unfeeling as real. This attitude to images leads others to start to place their trust in them.[1] This critique may equate too simply the work of religious craftsmen and the gods they seek to portray. But perhaps this sprang from observing the behaviour of such people and of the adherents of such deities.

While these prophets continued to believe in their own God, what they have introduced here is a quite extraordinary historical development in attitudes towards religion. It is the first time we come across a declaration that other nations create their own gods and that consequently these are "not gods" at all.[2]

It was the major prophets of the sixth century BC who articulated this critique most fully. Since their country had been conquered and most of its populace exiled, they were confronted more directly with foreign religions. As a result they came to have a more profound grasp of the man-made character of these gods. This was particularly the case with the following three prophets.

1. Jeremiah adds some vivid descriptive and comic touches.[3] Since the Israelites' gods cannot speak or act they are worthless, deceitful, and of human rather than divine origin.[4] Instead of basing his views on descriptions of how they are made, Jeremiah throws out a range of highly satirical questions and analogies. This springs, he says, from a loss of memory of the real God's character and uniqueness.[5] He is also the first to suggest that by engaging in worship of these man-made creations their followers run the risk of losing their sanity and humanity.[6]

2. Ezekiel underlines the irony in people making these gods out of the real God's own "most beautiful of jewels" of gold and silver, and then sacrificing their own sons to them.[7] He argues that this false religious behaviour stems from blurring the distinction between creature and creator.[8] This drains their worshippers of any vital spiritual life and divides them from their real selves.[9]

3. The author of Isaiah 40–66, who lived among the exiles in Babylonia, ridicules foreign gods more than any other Old Testament writer. Despite the apparent victory of foreign deities over Israel, he laughs their makers and worshippers to scorn.[10] He also notes how rivalries between these made-up gods divide people's religious allegiance. His final judgment is that

"they are all a delusion" and "their deeds amount to nothing".[11] They are merely a projection of people's own blindness.[12]

The importance of this breakthrough in religious insight is highly significant. Here, for the first time, the possibility of humans creating gods comes to expression. Even if the emphasis is more on physically manufacturing rather than mentally constructing gods, it implies the latter. Some of the ideas that appear in related modern critiques also begin to be hinted at. For example, how worshipping these gods unconsciously deflects what is essentially human onto what is imaginarily divine; how it leads to less rather than more genuine life and spirituality; how it results in loss of sanity and humanity. For these prophets, this is the very opposite of what belief in the real God should do.

A few post-biblical Jewish writers up to and beyond the beginning of the Christian era also take up this theme. While they possess greater literary excellence, and are more detailed, they generally contain less depth and passion. Only two works add something new.

First, the *Letter of Jeremiah*, a second- to fourth-century BC fictional letter modelled after the biblical prophet's "Letter to the Exiles" in Jeremiah 29, devotes itself to this. The author provides a wittier and fuller description of the manufacture, installation, and worship of foreign man-made gods than anything up to this point. In doing so he portrays them as totally dependent on human beings for their presentation and protection. His constant refrain is that "we have no evidence whatever that they are gods".[13]

Second, around the time of Christ, Philo, the great Jewish philosopher in Alexandria (30 BC – AD 45), brings a greater depth to the idea by drawing on earlier Jewish and

Greek ideas. He describes the creation of such gods by their makers as stemming from human "fancy", and as spreading "ignorance", "blindness", and "mischief" as to what is really true. This makes them worse than "a witless infant"; in fact "demented".[14] Elsewhere he includes the poets in his critique for their part in helping to deceive the people.[15] While Philo's portrait draws on earlier Jewish writings, his diagnosis of man-made religion as stemming from a failure of vision rather than of will shows the influence of Greek ideas, to which we now turn.

The first Greek critics

The first Greek critics of religion began to express their views shortly after the writings of the major Jewish prophets mentioned above.[16] During the sixth and fifth centuries BC, the traditional Olympian religion began to lose its hold on some aristocratic Athenian citizens. A small number of poets and philosophers began to question popular views of the gods. Several of these were subjected to investigation, accused of heresy, and occasionally even brought to trial.

Though this pantheon occupied the central place in public worship, the average person tended to rely more on one of the minor deities or fertility gods for help because of their greater emotional appeal and practical value. Only the mystery religions of Dionysius and Eleusis, partly drawn into the official cult, contained some of the same attraction.

The traditional gods also began to come under attack for their intellectual inadequacies. A few philosophers had already shifted their interest away from the role of gods in mythical stories, supernatural events, and everyday life and instead towards the search for a single rational principle at the

heart of the universe. These talked more about divinity than
deities, physical causes rather than the divine interventions,
invisible forces rather than tangible images. This ultimately
led "to a consciousness of the problem of religion itself – the
problem of accounting for the universal dispersion of the
idea of God and of discovering its sources".[17]

A forerunner of these critics was Xenophanes (570–478
BC), a poet-philosopher from Ionia. In surviving fragments
of his writings, he queries whether natural causes lie behind
extraordinary divine phenomena and denounces the immoral
and excessive behaviour of the gods. He also remarks on
variations in the way gods were popularly depicted:

> *Ethiopians make their gods snub-nosed and black;*
> *the Thracians make theirs blue-eyed and red-haired*
> *… Mortals imagine that the gods are begotten,*
> *and that the gods wear clothes like their own and*
> *have language and form like the voice and form of*
> *mortals. But if oxen or lions had hands and could*
> *draw and do the work with their hands that men*
> *do, horses would have drawn the form of gods like*
> *horses and oxen gods like oxen and they would*
> *represent the bodies of the gods just like their own*
> *forms.*[18]

Though these remarks sound sceptical about any idea
of gods, Xenophanes still believed in the divine. He did
this distinguishing between the firm knowledge of the
unchanging, refined divine nature and unreliable opinions
about changeable conceptions of the gods. Plato probably
had something similar in mind when he complained about
those of his predecessors who advocated that "the gods are
human contrivances, they do not exist in nature but only by

custom and law, which moreover differ from place to place according to the agreement made by each group when they laid down their laws".[19]

A century later the philosopher Democritus (c. 460–370 BC) arose during a period when Athens was coming to terms with the wider cultural life of Greece. As a result, earlier beliefs and practices came under greater scrutiny. Like Xenophanes, he distinguished between what he termed genuine knowledge and conventional knowledge. He placed "images" of the gods in the latter category, and identified a psychological motive in their formation. It was as men of old experienced fear of extraordinary phenomena that "perceiving these images, [they] imagined that each was a god, although God in reality is only that which has imperishable nature".[20] While they were mistaken in doing this, he believed that the gods were more than the products of human imagination, for an imperishable emanation of the divine still existed within them.

Another philosopher, Prodicus (c. 470–400 BC), also identified that a psychological motive was at work, but for him this was gratitude rather than fear. Though he was included in a list of "atheists", other indications suggest he too probably believed there was a genuine religious dimension to the gods.[21]

Around the same time the Athenian playwright-poet Critias (c. 460–403) has the leading character in his play *Sisyphus*, promoting a related idea. Rather than men in general,

> ... *a man of shrewd and subtle mind invented for men the fear of the gods, so that there might be something to frighten the wicked even if they acted, spoke or thought in secret. From this motive he*

introduced the notion of divinity. There is, he said, a
spirit enjoying endless life, hearing and seeing with
his mind, exceeding wise and all-observing, bearer
of a divine nature. He will hear everything spoken
among men and can see everything that is done.[22]

For this speaker, religion is a man-made illusion to maintain social and political control. If his words express more than a hypothetical point of view, this would be the first unmistakably atheist statement that we have. But as the speech occurs in a class of poetry that was allowed considerable dramatic liberty, and on the lips of a character who was a legendary type of criminal, we need to be cautious.

One other approach to religion from around this time requires mention. This argued that the gods were not imaginary creations of human beings but actual people whom they deified. Euhemerus (c. 340–260 BC) wrote a piece of travel fiction about an imaginary voyage to an unmapped island in the Indian Ocean. On the island a sacred inscription was discovered that recounted the history of the gods. The Olympian deities were identified as men who were venerated as gods because of their strength, intelligence, and achievements.[23] Over the next two millennia this "euhemeristic" account, as it was generally known, became one of the standard views of the origins of religion.

Later Jewish and Greek developments

After the destruction of the Temple towards the end of the first century AD, Judaism tended to focus inwards on strengthening its historical identity and core traditions more than on critiquing pagan religions and philosophies. The challenge of alternative man-made religions was no longer regarded as significant. Here and there the writings that dominate this period mention it, but the only extensive treatment is one tractate in the Mishnah (the first collection of oral Jewish teachings) and Talmud (a compendium of interpretations of these and other teachings), from the second and fourth centuries AD respectively. In the following centuries more mystical preoccupations tended to dominate.

Among the Greeks and then the Romans in this period, a range of poets, philosophers, and writers discussed the nature and importance of religion. As well as being influenced by the Greek thinkers mentioned above, these were affected by the wider exposure to foreign religions that resulted from ongoing military conquests. The practice of traditional religion continued during this time, though in a form characterized by assimilating the Greek and Roman pantheons. There were different gods for different needs and these penetrated all aspects of life. Meanwhile, foreign mystery religions also grew in influence by providing a more individual religious experience and exhibiting more regional adaptations in various parts of the empire. While some of the Roman writers show interest in the origin of religion, mostly they concentrate on more pressing issues such as divine providence and superstition.

Those like Cicero, Seneca, and Pliny, who occasionally discussed the origin of religion, mostly echoed or systematized earlier Greek views, especially those of Prodicus and Critias. Nevertheless they still maintained the practical necessity of belief in the divine. Where they attempted any psychological analysis, they were more interested in why people continued to adhere to gods rather than in whether those gods were illusory in character. Overall their views were less questioning than those of the philosophers who preceded them. In the final few centuries of Roman dominance, reflections on religion moved in more mystical and metaphysical directions.

The only figure of any interest from the Jewish or pagan side between the end of the Roman empire and the beginning of the early modern period was the Jewish philosopher Moses Maimonides (born around AD 1135). His main contribution was twofold. First, to insist that the critique of man-made religion was the most basic principle in the Law,[24] and this enabled some to manipulate and control people's allegiance. Second, to argue that since the foreign deities that confronted Israel had disappeared, man-made religion now arose as a challenge within monotheism itself. This crucial shift took place as people began to define God in humanlike terms by giving him a physical form, personal attributes, and psychic emotions.[25] He regarded this as a greater error than early pagan idolatry.[26] Maimonides also insisted that God could only be defined negatively, by what he is not rather than by what he is.

As we shall see, in the following period this opened the door to a more impersonal understanding of God and ultimately to a denial of his existence. Before considering how this happened, we need to step back a little to examine the contribution of Christianity to the view that humankind created the gods.

3

Its Later Uptake
and Turnaround

We have looked at how 2,500 years ago two groups of thinkers came up with the idea that many gods were manmade. Jewish prophets said this about all *foreign gods* whose images were worshipped by the nations around them; Greek philosophers said it about *popular gods* who were worshipped in many local communities. The former made this criticism in the name of one universal God and the latter on the basis of an impersonal conception of the divine. There were continuing, at times merging, echoes of these views during the following centuries among several Roman thinkers. After that it was Christian writers, mainly building on a Jewish foundation but partly influenced by Greek and Roman ideas, who further developed this critique.

Christianity was born into a more cosmopolitan religious world than its predecessors. By this time the official public religion had fused the Greek and Roman pantheons. This spread as the Roman empire expanded and, especially in the East, was accompanied by divine veneration of the emperor. As the official cult no longer gripped most people's allegiance, mystery cults imported by merchants, soldiers, migrants, and slaves became more popular, especially in the army and among some of the aristocracy.

By the third century AD, a range of intellectuals and politicians were actively promoting the rites of such deities as Attis, Cybele, Isis and Osiris, and later, Mithras. As many artists and craftsmen were employed in producing statues and cultic objects for these, such religions were economically as well as religiously important. Where Christian writers had been converted as adults, they knew something of the official cult in which they once participated. Though some had been exposed to one or other of the mystery religions, mostly their knowledge of them was second-hand.

The early Christian contribution to the idea

Jesus never refers to the people outside of Israel creating gods in their own image. Although he talks about how people add human traditions to divine revelation, Jesus' silence on this matter probably stems from his living almost wholly within the borders of Palestine. Jesus never refers to the people creating gods in their own image. The apostle Paul, who travelled widely in the ancient world, was the first to do this, though only briefly in three places.

Arriving in Athens during his last missionary journey Paul describes images of the gods that are set up in the marketplace as the product of "man's design or skill" and being placed in man-made temples.[1] He views this partly as the result of ignorance arising from their suppression of the truth about God's power and deity revealed in creation, and partly as the influence of demons playing on people's evil tendencies. The "so-called" gods they worship are in reality "nothing".[2]

During the following four centuries, a number of early apologists for the Christian faith further developed these ideas. Apart from the author of the early second-century *Letter to Diognetus*, who reflects primarily a prophetic point of view, others combine elements of earlier Jewish and Greek ideas on the origin of the gods. For Justin (c. AD 100–165), gods were invented because people feared apparitions and because they wanted to deify respected leaders.[3] This was a similar view to that held by his pupil Tatian (c. AD 110–172) and Athenagoras, a converted philosopher (c. AD 133–190), who, interestingly, defends Christians against being charged as atheists simply because they do not believe in the official gods.[4]

The more profound Christian thinkers that followed also refer to the role of demons in persuading people to invent gods, but they also add new elements to the view that essentially the gods were a human creation. In preliminary ways, these sometimes anticipate more modern views on the subject. Between them they explored the motives that lay at the root of this process more extensively, proposed a more comprehensive analysis and framework, and delved more deeply into the psychological motives at work.

The first of these, Clement (c. AD 150–211/216) from Alexandria, draws on the views of the Jewish prophets as well as on several Greek and Roman thinkers. While he leaves the precise relationship of human and demonic contributions to making gods unclear, he provides a more detailed list of the *underlying causes* involved than anything yet offered. These include:

- fear of punishment, such as divinizing of calamity;

- idealizing of emotions, such as fear, love, joy, hope;

- deifying notable aspects of life, such as justice.[5]

Significant here is Clement's recognition that the origin of the gods did not have its basis in any single cause but in a complex set of psychological, cognitive, and imaginative factors.

His student Lactantius (AD 240–320), a teacher of rhetoric, investigates pagan religion in a more matter-of-fact way, explores its motivations more fully, and provides the most comprehensive analysis up to his time. While he traces the origin of the Greek gods to the deifying of men, and criticizes the Roman divinizing of specific events and virtues, he views the image worship associated with the mystery religions as both childish and crazy.[6] He also delves more deeply into the psychological factors involved and does so in a way that foreshadows more sophisticated modern ideas. The motive was to draw people back

> *into favour with themselves, that they may not …*
> *greatly despise themselves, nor think that they are*
> *weak and useless, and of no account … [but so*
> *that] they would value themselves highly, and would*
> *understand that there is more in man than appears.*[7]

Lactantius recognized that some pagan philosophers knew the errors involved in this, and as such he felt they deserved less respect than the common people, who falsely believed the gods to be real.[8]

One of the best-known early theologians, Athanasius (c. AD 296–373), was Egyptian by birth, Greek by education, and Christian by conviction. His first work, *Against the Heathen*, a defence of Christianity for educated people, provides a more intellectually profound discussion of the origin of the gods than those of his predecessors. The first humans preferred the attractions of the senses rather than those of the mind, and a love of self more than love of God. This led them to start imagining false and illusory ideas.[9] As a result, the soul

> *weighed down with all fleshly desire, and distracted among the impressions of these things, imagines that the God whom her understanding has forgotten is to be found in bodily and sensible things … Having learned to contrive evil, which is no reality in itself, in like manner feigned for themselves as gods beings that had no real existence.*[10]

With minor differences to Clement, Athanasius lists the various stages of degeneration this passed through as people created gods to match the variety of their passions.[11]

The following period adds only minor developments in this critique of the gods. Arnobius (died c. AD 330) introduces a more personal note by referring to the way he once, as a pagan, held "fanciful beliefs, so that they fashioned gods after themselves, and gave to these such a nature as they have themselves, in actions, circumstances and desires".[12] In the following century the battle against idolatry was largely completed throughout the empire.

Augustine's (AD 354–430) greatest apologetic work, *The City of God*, is less interested in discussing the birth of the gods than in helping to bury them. A novel observation was in discerning that the human tendency to make God in our own image remains a factor for many who become Christians. For "it was easier for people to drive out idols from their sacred buildings than to drive them out of their minds and imaginations".[13]

The later Christian contribution

This idea became a repeated theme centuries later in the Protestant Reformation's protest against the medieval church (1517–55). The leading reformer in Germany, Martin Luther (1483–1546), believed that in his day the human tendency to create God in its image was more sophisticated than in biblical times and more rampant than in previous centuries. But much of his critique was directed at false substitutes for the worship of God, for: "Whatever you hang your heart upon and trust, that is actually your God."[14] In this way art, power, cleverness, favour, money, friendship, even marriage, could become substitute gods. Those who call themselves Christians are as capable of this as others.

The remainder of Luther's critique was directed at false worship in the church, and at those who "invent things in accordance with their own ideas ... a god to suit [their] own opinion ... They worship the figment of their imagination more truly than the true God, for they believe that the latter is like their imagination."[15]

These remarks did not lead on to any general discussion of ways in which the idea of God was made over by believers. More significant for the later discussion of how human beings created every version of God, including the Christian one, was the highly emphatic way Luther sometimes spoke about faith itself as actually generating belief in God.

His younger contemporary in France, and then Switzerland, John Calvin (1509–64), had a generally similar approach. For him "man's nature is a perpetual factory of idols".[16] He refers here mainly to the mental not physical creation of false images of God, which he found pervasive in Roman Catholic thinking. More explicitly than Luther he traces this tendency back to the beginnings of the human race.

> *Daily experience teaches us that flesh is always uneasy until it has obtained some figment like itself in which it may fondly find solace as an image of God. In almost every age since the beginning of the world men, in order that they might obey this blind desire, have set up symbols in which they believe God appeared before their bodily eyes ... We must not think the heathen so stupid that they did not understand God to be something other than sticks and stones. For while they change images at pleasure, they always kept the same gods in mind.*[17]

During the next two centuries, especially among Puritan writers inspired by the reformers, only a few paid any substantial attention to this issue and did so mainly for practical reasons. They were less interested in explaining how man-made religion arose than in identifying its characteristics and effects. Like William Perkins (1558–1602), mostly they preferred "not to enter on the dispute, whether all their oracles were mere delusions of men, or whether they were real abuses of the devil himself".[18] Few were interested in the psychological processes involved in people forming false conceptions of God.

One of these, Richard Sibbes (1557–1635), located the problem in their imaginations, which he viewed as bordering between the senses and understanding, and driven by pleasure rather than truth. It is this that transforms God into a figure we manufacture for ourselves, who fits in with our own preferences, and leads to our living in a dream-like fantasy. For him, satanic as well as human activity is involved in this and only dependence on revelation and reason can correct it, for: "We should not bring God down to our imaginations but raise our imaginations up to God."[19]

Where these writers did display an interest in the issue, it was with the appearance of what they called "atheism". This term began to come into vogue in the late sixteenth century. Initially it referred more to those who believed in God but lived as they wished, and to those who challenged traditional religious beliefs and practices, than to the small number who denied the existence of God altogether. In particular, these writers attacked criticisms of depictions of God as a vital person engaging intimately with his creatures rather than as a distant deity, arguing that since humankind was made in the image of God this was quite improper. In part this was a reaction against the opposite tendency to describe God in purely human terms.

The rationalist religious shift

This was influenced in part by the renewed interest in classical religions that was taking place in the sixteenth and seventeenth centuries. This reminded people of the all too recognizably human attitudes and actions of the Greek and Roman gods. These deities were essentially human beings writ large. It was also partly influenced by reports of current pagan religions brought back by travellers to foreign lands. The exotic accounts they provided of continuing pagan beliefs and rites fascinated people who lived in more civilized societies. Two questions these provoked were:

1. How could the apparent similarities between ancient and modern heathens be accounted for?

2. How could the apparent similarities between pagan rituals and certain Jewish and Christian practices be accounted for?

Traditional Christian thinkers argued that an original belief in one God had been destroyed by humankind's fall into sin, as a result of which false religions arose and even true religion could be corrupted. Other thinkers who significantly modified Christian beliefs, such as the Deists, developed a less personal view of God and a more naturalistic account of how superstition developed out of an original monotheism. For them the essence of true religion in all times and places shifted to what lay at the heart of Jesus' life and teaching. The challenge for them was no longer advocating the superiority of Christianity over Judaism and Islam, but defending religion itself against those who regarded it inessential to being human.

In this discussion there was a revival of classical critiques of the birth of the gods, especially those of Prodicus and Euhemerus (see earlier discussions in Chapter 2). Historical and psychological accounts of how this happened were preferred over reference to demonic influence. Less emphasis was placed on human wilfulness and sin, and more on human frailty and error, occasionally linked with mental aberration. There was a tendency to see the origin of religion as part of the childhood of the human race, and then its development in a more sophisticated direction.

There were two other significant aspects of this general shift in approach. First, the rational defence or naturalistic interpretation of religion was discussed in a more analytical way and was based on reason more than revelation. Second, the move to describing God negatively in terms of what he is not rather than by means of human analogies opened up the possibility of a more radical critique of God's existence.

The most significant discussions that followed originated with three significant representatives of this rationalist tradition. The first was Pierre Bayle (1647–1706), who revived in France the fear theory of the origins of religion, especially emphasizing anxiety about the future. Though Bayle presented himself as an orthodox believer, some of his comments anticipate later diagnoses of religious experience along psychopathological lines:

> A religious mania is like a dream. In sleep too the mind proliferated fantasies in response to inner illumination by the memory of weird legends or grotesque myths … The imagination will then be stronger than sight and will depict its objects as present, so that even while awake, one will believe that one sees something that is not before one's eyes, but is apparent only to the inner senses … The same thing can happen to those who are not asleep if, by the effect of some fear or some powerful internal emotion, the acts of the emotion have greater power than that of sight or hearing.[20]

Bayle influenced the substantive psychological theories of influential English Deists like the earl of Shaftesbury, who added a physiological basis to Bayle's approach. Meanwhile Bayle's fellow-countryman Bernard de Fontanelle (1657–1757) built on the fear theory of religious origins, but placed more emphasis on the cognitive rather than psychological errors involved.

The second significant representative of this tradition was David Hume (1711–76), who developed a more full-blown "Natural History of Religion". He moved from a merely sceptical attitude to the arguments for the existence of God to inherent suspicion of the personal motivations behind these. His investigation of the nature and limits of human understanding provided a schema outlining popular attitudes towards religion down through the ages. Dismissing the idea of innate, or cognitive, religious sentiments, Hume viewed human emotions as the seat of primitive beliefs. In doing this he made three innovations. First, it was the objects of their *hopes* as well as *fears*, associated with their self-interested feelings of pleasure and pain, that people reified. Second, though this was not primarily a rational exercise, it was as humans distinguished between their nobler and baser characteristics that they projected their intelligence onto illusory deities. Third, this resulted in an original polytheism rather than monotheism.

Even when the idea of one God arose it did not spring from reason but from

> ... *the perpetual hopes and fears, wishes and apprehensions. By degrees, the acute imagination of men, uneasy in this abstract conception of objects, about which it is incessantly employed, begins to render them more particular, and to clothe them in shapes more suitable to its natural comprehension. It represents them to be sensible, intelligent beings,*

> *like mankind; actuated by love and hatred, and*
> *flexible by gifts and entreaties, by prayers and*
> *sacrifices. Hence the origin of religion and hence*
> *the origin of idolatry or polytheism. But the same*
> *anxious concern for happiness ... allows mankind*
> *not to remain for long in the first simple conception*
> *of them; as powerful but limited beings ... elevating*
> *their deities to the utmost bonds of perfection, at last*
> *begets the attributes of unity, and infinity, simplicity*
> *and spirituality.*[21]

Hume allowed a secondary place for divinizing men rather than inventing gods, and believed that instead of polytheism tending to develop into monotheism, after a time monotheism generally fell back into polytheism. At the end of this work, expanding on his reference to "sick men's dreams", Hume provided a detailed description of the manic-depressive nature of belief in his *Dialogues Concerning Natural Religion* (1779). Ultimately, however much he inclined to an agnostic rather than atheist perspective, his whole approach undermined the basis of previous rational apologies for revealed religion and therefore of Christianity itself.

The extreme rationalist critique

The final representative of this movement was Paul-Henri d'Holbach (1723–89), who took the final step into a fully rationalist and anti-religious position. He produced the most aggressive attack yet upon the reality and morality of belief in God. For him, there was little distinction between religions, including Christianity. He was willing to employ any argument, even at the expense of logical consistency, to discredit them. Religion was not just a mistake, fantasy or mania, but a disease that had spread like a pestilence throughout the world. The origin of the gods in primitive times lay in primitive man's fear of nature's unpredictability and life's painful misfortunes. These gradually became ingrained in our personal and institutional memory of past catastrophes. In early childhood people relied upon parents to allay these fears, then upon others around them who were stronger, and in adulthood took refuge in a fictional divine being.

The form this fear took in each individual shaped the specific character of their personal god:

> Man never judges those objects of which he is ignorant except through the medium of those which come within his knowledge: thus man, taking himself for the model, ascribed will, intelligence, design, projects, passions: in a word, qualities analogous to his own, to all those unknown causes of which he experienced the action ... He attributes views, plans, a system of conduct like his own to everything which to his limited ideas appears of itself to produce connected effects, to act with regularity, to constantly operate in the same manner, that uniformly produces the same sensations in every person.[22]

Alongside these tutelary gods, societies also created national gods for themselves by deifying their first lawmakers, inventors and religious geniuses or, on occasions, adopted the god of a conquering people. Such gods, reflecting man's own fearful nature, included the Jewish God, a suspicious tyrant who demanded animal sacrifice and exacted revenge on his enemies. The Christian God only managed to surmount this by appeasing himself through the arranged death of his Son.

It is not so much the content of his critique but the volatility of his attack and the brazenness of his atheism that sets d'Holbach apart from his predecessors. While built on earlier theories, his emphasis on the role of pain in inducing fear was novel. He was also the first to coin the term "anthropomorphism" for attributing human emotions to the gods. His emphasis on the way people hold on to infantile religious attitudes in an anxiety-ridden, obsessive way also anticipated Sigmund Freud. D'Holbach maintained that people could only overcome these illusory beliefs through the dispassionate study of religion's origins, nature, and effects. In part the seeds for this belief were sown in the earlier Deist view that the distinctive element in religion was cognitively irrelevant,[23] but its full flowering is embedded in his thoroughly eighteenth-century Enlightenment treatment.

When reading the writings of the New Atheists, it is d'Holbach who most quickly comes to mind. Their aggressive attitude, no-holds-barred approach, inflammatory style, dismissive comments on everything to do with religion, and flaunting of their atheism, all hark back to his extreme attack on Christianity. A further example of this is the less well-known book, *Then Man Created God* by D. G. McLeod.[24] In this sense both he and they step back from the more complex and substantive critiques of religion that will come before us next.

Looking back over this all-too-brief survey of the view that religion is an imaginary man-made creation, we see several stages in its development.

- In the earliest Jewish and Greek thinkers the target was primarily foreign deities or popular religion from the perspective of belief in God or a more impersonal notion of divinity.

- Among Roman and then early Christian writers there was a broadening and maturing of this critique.

- In later Christian writers we begin to see it directed at some of their official beliefs and practices within their own religion, and in Deist writers at expressions of folk religion and religious belief more widely.

- With d'Holbach we are on the brink of a more radical viewpoint. This is an overt attack upon Judaism and Christianity themselves as purely man-made religions, followed by their reinterpretation in humanist terms or prediction of their demise.

In the last point the initial rejection of false gods as human creations has been turned completely on its head. It has become a rejection of the very God from whom the original critique was said to have come. This was quite a breathtaking development and is nothing less than one of the most striking reversals of thought in human history.

PART THREE

FOUR LEADING
MODERN APPROACHES

4

GOD AS THE PRODUCT OF HUMAN WISHES

Ludwig Feuerbach

We now come to the four main modern approaches to the view that God is a human-made creation by examining the writings of their leading exponents and their more recent followers. This begins in mid-nineteenth-century Germany, where reflection on religion followed a different course to what was happening elsewhere. As we have seen, in England a more rational post-Reformation approach to the evidences for Christianity ended, in Hume, with an agnostic Deism. In France, the more sceptical monotheism of Bayle ended in d'Holbach, with outright materialistic atheism.

In Germany, although the philosopher Hegel's (1770–1831) system centred on the idea of God-in-the-making, the real discussion was about humanity's desire to realize itself and fulfil its godlike potential. A dramatic expression of this was the character of Faust in Goethe's famous poem of the same name.

Instead of God as the one who created the world, entered it in the incarnation, and restored it to a right relationship with himself, Hegel's system recounts the story of "God-in-the-making", who incorporates the world into himself, becoming fully self-conscious and divine in the process. The most radical element in this view is that it is in and through human, especially philosophical, reflection that this development of God takes place.

In the decade after Hegel's death, his followers split into two camps. Those on the more conservative right held to a more theological Christianized interpretation of his views. Those on the more radical left, convinced that the question "What is God?" had been resolved as "God is Man", sought to work out what this meant in practice. The most influential early representative of this latter movement was a young German philosopher, Ludwig Feuerbach (1804–72), who took this system to its logical conclusion. By thoroughly recasting Hegel, Feuerbach formulated the first comprehensive critique of God in particular and Christianity in general as a humanly created illusion.

Feuerbach himself summed up what he understood to be his particular contribution:

> *Christianity reproached heathenism for idolatry.*
> *Protestantism reproached Catholicism ... for*
> *idolatry, and Rationalism now reproaches ... the*
> *older orthodox Protestantism for idolatry, because it*
> *worships a man as God, and therefore an image of*
> *God ... in place of the original ... real being. But I*
> *go further and say: Rationalism itself, indeed every*
> *religion and cult which sets up a God, i.e., an unreal*
> *being, a being different and separate from real*
> *nature ... and which makes it an object of worship,*
> *is the worship of images and consequently idolatry.*[1]

Feuerbach's background is interesting. The son of an eminent jurist and raised in a nominally Lutheran household, he studied Hebrew with a rabbi during his teenage years. In his early twenties, his religious inclinations led him to study theology under Friedrich Schleiermacher (1768–1834), the first so-called "modern" theologian. The latter sought to safeguard Christianity from sceptical attacks by basing knowledge of God on human consciousness rather than on reason. But on hearing Hegel's lectures, Feuerbach's interests began to shift toward philosophy. Over time he found his new mentor's reinterpretation of Christianity too abstract and idealized; it needed to be down to earth. While still wanting to uphold the essence of religion, especially Christianity, he argued that this involved distinguishing between its illusory theological form and substantive human content.

Feuerbach began to do this in a preliminary work, *Thoughts on Death and Immortality* (1830). Christianity, he asserted, was a kind of illusory insurance policy against the fear and fact of mortality. After completing a history of philosophy that underlined the importance of, among others, Pierre Bayle, he wrote his groundbreaking *The Essence of Christianity* (1841). This immediately became the most talked about book in Germany and was so popular that it went through three revisions in the next seven years. It was also translated into French and English, the latter by the famous novelist George Eliot.

Three years after the book's release, Feuerbach issued a brief supplement entitled *The Essence of Faith According to Luther* (1844). This was followed by a brief discussion, *The Essence of Religion* (1846), and the more wide-ranging *Lectures on the Essence of Religion* (1851). Finally came his study of Greek religion in *The Theogony* (1857).

Feuerbach's inversion of Christianity

Though Feuerbach was basically preoccupied with humankind, he worked out his understanding of this primarily through exploring religion. As a fundamental expression of what it is to be human, religion

> is the dream of the human mind. But even in dreams we do not find ourselves in emptiness or in heaven, but on earth in the realm of reality; we only see real things in the entrancing splendour of imagination and caprice instead of seeing them in the simple daylight of reality and necessity. Hence I do nothing more to religion – and to speculative philosophy and theology – than to open its eyes … i.e., I change the object as it is in the imagination to the object in reality.[2]

This takes place through recognizing that "in every wish we find concealed a god, but in or behind every god there lies concealed nothing but a wish".[3] In religion men seek in heaven what they cannot find on earth. This is how they try to compensate for their helplessness, for the more empty life is the more full and real God is to them.

In Feuerbach's view, humankind has its origin in nature and is dependent both on it and upon others. Religion arises from humankind's awareness of dependence on nature. As people strive to liberate themselves from their physical dependence, they first begin to personify and worship nature and natural forces. This is how polytheism arose. In the next stage, as civilization develops, people become more aware of their dependence upon others as a moral necessity. According to their diverse needs they fashion objects of worship that vary from one society to another. Instead of personifying nature and natural forces, they now attribute personal and social attributes to what they worship. This is how the familiar gods of ancient cultures, including the Greek and Roman pantheons, arose.

As human needs changed, and as people realized the importance of reason and laws, their deities became less arbitrary and unpredictable. Though this gave them a greater sense of connection with the gods, and of their capacity to intervene in human affairs, it did not give them independence of, and mastery over, nature or others. For these reasons, such religion remained unsatisfactory. As their awareness developed:

> ... what an earlier religion regarded as objective, is now recognised as subjective; that is, what was formerly contemplated and worshipped as God is now perceived to be something human. What was at first religion becomes at a later period idolatry; man is seen to have adored his own nature ... every advance in religion is therefore a deeper self-knowledge. But every particular religion, while it announces its predecessors idolatrous, excepts itself – and necessarily so, otherwise it would no longer be religion.[4]

Monotheism does not appear until human beings have made themselves and their achievements the heart and goal of nature. Only then does the hope of liberation from nature find its fulfilment. Whereas polytheism sought to assuage man's fears by humanizing nature, monotheism seeks to subjugate nature to a divine being who reflects human nature. According to Feuerbach, the God of the Old

Testament was the first expression of this. But since it talks about a particular people, and God's actions focus only on their aspirations and needs, he is only ever a national God.

It is therefore in Christianity that the idea of a universal God first appears. In *The Essence of Christianity* Feuerbach's aim was to demonstrate that Christianity provided the supreme example of God being created in human likeness. Rather than, as with d'Holbach, simply demolishing Christianity, he argued that it should be reinterpreted and appropriated. For initially what we need to know about humankind can best be learned from it.

This is clear from the structure of the book, which first discusses the "true" aspects of religion and only then the "false" theological expressions of this that theology has developed. Christianity was superior to all other religions because for the first time its view of God embodied a universal understanding of humanity. Its belief that God becomes human conceals the deeper truth that humankind becomes God. The positive side of this is that man's powers, qualities and characteristics are so highly regarded that they are deified. The negative side is that these are projected into an independent spiritual realm that alienates them from their very human creators:

> *Man denies to himself only what he attributes to God ... God is the infinite, man the finite being; God is perfect, man imperfect; God eternal, man temporal; God almighty, man weak; God holy, man sinful. God and man are extremes: God is the absolutely positive, the sum of all realities; man the absolutely negative, comprehending all negations. But in religion man contemplates his own latent nature ... The fact is not that a quality is divine*

*because God has it but that God has it because it is
in itself divine, because without it God would be a
defective being.*[5]

In worshipping God, therefore, humankind unknowingly
and indirectly worships itself, failing to realize that the only
real gap is between individuals and their human essence, not
between them and God. It is only because God is represented
as having these human qualities that he is of interest to
humankind. For Feuerbach, the less personal God of the
Deists actually diminishes rather than refines religion. On the
other hand, the complete denial of God by aggressive atheists
attacks humanity as well as religion. A God who possesses
reason, will, and love is much more able to be reinterpreted as
a reflection of fundamental human characteristics.

Initially it was human reason that possessed
independence, unity, and boundlessness. Only after it became
aware of its weaknesses were these projected onto God.
Initially will was a purely human feature. It was only ascribed
to God so that he could act as well as think. Initially love was
only experienced between human beings. It was only when
God's demands made us aware of our moral inadequacy that
we infused him with love to help us overcome this. Only love
is able to reach down to us and draw us up to him. For it
is the mediator between "the perfect and the imperfect, the
sinless and the sinful, the universal and the individual, the
law and the heart, the divine and the human. Love is God
himself and outside it there is no God. Love makes man God
and God man."[6]

This is why the central religious symbol of Christianity
is the incarnation. Rather than being an extraordinary divine
intervention to save humankind, it is the natural conclusion
humans had to draw from the premises on which religion

was created. It was the Protestant, especially Lutheran, form of Christianity which most fully articulated the real human content of religion. In Feuerbach's supplementary essay *The Essence of Religion According to Luther*, he pointed to the reformer's insistence on the way God's desire sought to satisfy our longings and needs rather than focus upon himself, on religious devotion to God in himself, and on Christ's benefits for us rather than primarily on Christ himself. In other words it was the welfare of human beings that lay at the heart of the Christian religion. Feuerbach assembled a whole range of statements from Luther to support this view. In this book he shifted his earlier emphasis on human essence or human species more towards the concrete, physical individual.

In a similar vein, Feuerbach goes on to recast a number of major doctrines – including the Trinity, creation, revelation, miracles, and sacraments, as well as other Christian practices such as providence, prayer and faith – to bring out their essentially human substance.

- The doctrine of the *Trinity* is merely a reflection of the humanly desired trinity of reason, love, and will.

- The doctrine of *creation* speaks of our human capacity to imagine and create something out of nothing, so gratifying our desire to master nature and escape fate.

- The doctrine of *revelation* acknowledges that our thoughts and words are central to understanding our deepest desires and search for meaning.

- Faith in *miracles* is a celebration of the imaginative power of human fantasy and of personal wish-fulfilments over the laws of nature.

- Celebration of the *sacraments* is a ceremonial recognition of the divine healing power of nature and the divine nature of sensory objects.

Feuerbach also reinterprets several other Christian beliefs and practices such as providence, prayer, faith, resurrection and heaven.

So, then, religion is a wish-fulfilment that is born out of our frustrations and efforts to surmount them. Though it can offer us emotional comfort, the difficulty is that it is "more comfortable to be saved and freed by another than to free oneself … it is more comfortable to know that God loves one than to love oneself with that simple, natural self love which is innate to all beings".[7]

In its place Feuerbach wanted to "turn the lovers of God into lovers of men, the worshippers into workers, the candidates for the life to come into students of this present life, the Christians into complete men; he wanted to turn away from heaven towards earth, from faith towards love, from Christ towards ourselves, from all supernaturalism to real life".[8]

As the culprit is theology not religion, Feuerbach devotes the second half of *The Essence of Christianity* to attacking it. Theology's error is that it abstracts and objectifies what belongs to humankind onto God instead of reinterpreting what is divine into human terms. The so-called proofs of God's existence only compound this error.

In the form in which he presented it, Feuerbach's approach to religion had few imitators in the decades after his death. Given its widespread influence during his day, in one sense this is surprising, in another not.

On the one hand, radical thinkers like Marx believed that Feuerbach had essentially completed the criticism of religion and that it merely required modifying and extending in certain ideological ways. Later innovative thinkers like Freud largely took it for granted and sought to ground it psychologically and give it a more scientific basis.

On the other hand, those attracted by its humanist message were generally less interested in preserving its religious essence and investigating why particular ideas about God arose, and more interested in formulating arguments against the existence of God. Certainly no one reinterpreted a range of Christian doctrines in the way that Feuerbach did.

Strangely enough, in the long term it was ultimately theologians who endeavoured to do this. In Europe Fritz Buri (1907–95) believed that the only way to effectively communicate with unbelievers in a post-Second World War setting was to translate belief in God into non-theistic existential terms. In practice this meant dissolving God, divine grace, and redemption into the language of intense and grateful awareness of authentic existence. As a result, theology was fully merged with existential philosophy.[9] Something similar was attempted a little later in England by Don Cupitt (b. 1934), for whom God became primarily a symbol of human possibilities, and by the American theologian Paul van Buren (1924–88), who felt it was necessary to avoid referring to God altogether in trying to reach a post-religious age.[10] Though both these projects are very much in the spirit of Feuerbach, and in part update it for an existentialist or secularist audience respectively, they do not display the range, depth, passion, and rhetoric of his approach.

Evaluating Feuerbach's approach

1. His view of God

In view of Feuerbach's wholesale reinterpretation of how the idea of God came into being and how we should reinterpret it, it is appropriate to examine what he understands by the word "God". His portrait of God in the Old Testament as particularly the God of Israel is, of course, well documented. But Feuerbach pictures God in purely national terms. While this is only of secondary relevance to his main argument that human beings imagined God into being, it does tend to present a more limited view of God than appears in many of the biblical writings. This overlooks the wider picture presented in the opening chapters of Genesis, the writings of the major prophets, and the visions of later prophetic figures. In various ways all of these depict God as having a more global perspective. God is also portrayed as having more of a concern for the material world than Feuerbach's predominant focus on the human dimension.

More relevant to his main argument is his view of God in the New Testament. While he rightly regards the incarnation as central to Christianity, the role of the Father fades into the background and is overshadowed by the presence of the Son. This enables him to focus more exclusively on Jesus' human character and achievements, and interpret these as extensions of more general human aspirations and accomplishments. In other words, it helps him highlight the human, at the expense of the divine, dimension of early Christianity. However, since Feuerbach gives extensive attention to the nature of God elsewhere in his writings, his argument does not stand or fall merely on his treatment of Christ.

When Feuerbach turns to Luther, he certainly always quotes the reformer with accuracy. But he does not always do so in context or in the light of Luther's full contribution. He rightly brings out Luther's insistence on the role and power of faith in Christian belief, and also the significance he gives to "God-for-us" rather than "God-in-himself". But Luther focused on this in order to correct the current Roman Catholic over-emphasis on works and abstract medieval debates about God's nature. Though, unlike Calvin, he sometimes failed to safeguard the difference between the divine and the human, he did not do this as much as is sometimes suggested. So while Luther provides Feuerbach with some ammunition for his view that God is merely the idea of humanity writ large, he does not do this to the extent or with the intent that Feuerbach alleges.

To summarize: Feuerbach's treatment of God as portrayed in classical Jewish, early Christian, and later Protestant writings is partly biased towards his reinterpretation of Christianity. But in light of his wider discussion of God elsewhere in his writings, this limitation of itself is insufficient to invalidate the full thrust of his views.

2. His view of man

Since, for Feuerbach, it is we who have invented God in our image by transferring human characteristics to a divine being, the success of his inversion of the traditional Jewish and Christian belief depends heavily on his understanding of human nature. When he analyses the factors that generated religion, he variously cites people's wish-fulfilment, human dependence, what humankind admires, and self-knowledge. He also derives ideas of the divine transcendence variously from the human search to transcend nature, human understanding, and the human species regarded from the point of view of the individual. Presumably to some degree or other all of these have a role in its origin and development. His varying statements on these factors are not in themselves therefore a sign of confusion in his thinking. Where we do find a problem, however, is in his tendency to slide between talking about human nature in individual terms and talking about it in terms of the human species as a whole.

Overall Feuerbach is still too wedded to a general idea of Man, or the human race, at the expense of the individual. This happens despite his desire to relate his approach to human beings in an empirical rather than abstract way. His basic argument about how the idea of God arose and matured forces him in this direction, for the full human potentialities he regards humanity as ascribing to God do not make sense if they only spring from limited individuals. No individual or group of individuals possesses all the qualities and characteristics imprinted by humans upon God. In particular it is hard to make sense of the traditional divine attributes – such as God's infinity, omniscience and omnipresence – as a reflection of concrete individuals. Quite apart from this, to portray these as dimensions of the human species is scarcely any more persuasive in the long run.

There is a real weakness in Feuerbach here – one that stems from his view of human nature but ultimately subverts his view of God as a human invention. In addition, Feuerbach never asked why human beings should create a divine double of themselves to satisfy their unfulfilled longings and fears. This only makes sense if there is some further contradiction of which we are unaware or that we are unwilling to acknowledge. It was left to others who came after him, such as Marx and Freud, to try and remedy this defect.

3. His view of wishes and longings

The role human wishes and longings play in Feuerbach's account overlooks a basic issue. As C. S. Lewis pointed out, whether or not we wish for something tells us nothing about whether the object of our wish is true. To think otherwise is to judge the truth of an idea by the feelings and thoughts we have of it. This, says Lewis, is illogical: "Some of the things I would like to believe must in fact be true; it is impossible to arrange a universe which contradicts everyone's wishes, in every respect, at every moment."[11] Indeed, the prevalence of such a wish that there be a God in so many people down through the ages could be just as much a sign that it corresponds to the truth.

In support of his overall position here, Lewis argues that the general wishes of human beings – such as the infant crying for food, the lover longing for sex, the curious longing for knowledge – all have their counterparts in the real world. With respect to religion, he also suggests that it is difficult to reduce some responses, such as the overwhelming awareness of awesome spiritual realities or the centrality of sacrificing oneself for others, simply to wish-fulfilment. Many, Lewis himself among them, have had the experience of being inexorably pursued, confronted and challenged by God in a way that ran quite counter to their personal preferences.

In this way, the kind of God the Bible talks about is *not* the kind one would naturally wish for. This is why, when he eventually came to faith, Lewis described the moment as one where: "At last I fell to my knees and admitted that God was God – perhaps, at that moment, the most dejected and reluctant convert in all England."[12]

Feuerbach's two-sided legacy

In concluding this treatment of Feuerbach, two things may be said about his ambiguous legacy. The first has to do with his ultimate picture of God. Overall it comes through as rather abstract. This is because one of the difficulties in Feuerbach's analysis of religion is his undeclared but continuing debt to Hegel. While he seeks to invert Hegel by overtly focusing on the centrality of humankind rather than God, his understanding of Christianity is still shaped by Hegel's philosophical recasting of a more dynamic biblical view of God. In this respect it is very different from the picture that comes through in the writings of his contemporary Søren Kierkegaard (1813–55). In these God has a vital, often surprising, personal but more-than-human character that is directly based on the earliest Christian writings. More recent efforts by theologians like Van Harvey (b. 1926) to save Feuerbach by identifying a thread in his writings on which to build a more positive religious perspective are still too removed from a lively, personal view of God to be very appealing.[13]

On the other hand, according to Karl Barth, the twentieth century's most famous theologian, "no philosopher of his time penetrated the contemporary theological situation as well as he, and few spoke with such pertinence".[14]

It was Barth's view that the theology of Feuerbach's day had so compromised the central importance of God's identity and revelation in favour of man's self-consciousness and experience, that it lay exposed to his humanistic interpretation. In doing this it had opened a door that Feuerbach simply walked right through. He laid bare the basic weakness of any approach to God that worked from humankind upwards rather than God downwards. Whoever began from this starting point – whether ordinary seeker, typical believer or Christian thinker – ended up in the same position. All were unable to defend themselves against creating a view of God that reflected their own needs and aspirations. This is why, for Barth, Feuerbach is "the thorn in the flesh of modern theology".[15]

A final challenge to Feuerbach concerns several of his basic premises. First, his view that rationality is the most basic characteristic of what it is to be human. If this is the case, our main problem is overcoming false thinking, not false acting. Here Feuerbach is a true son of the Enlightenment. However important reasoning may be to human beings, the capacity to love others in a profound way – and for believers, loving God – is more fundamental.

Second, his assumption that God does not exist. It is only after taking this for granted that he asks how belief in God arose. But logically it is just as reasonable to enquire why disbelief in God arose. Instead of belief in God arising from our mistaken need for dependence, one could argue that disbelief in God springs from our mistaken sense of autonomy. Independently of reason, Feuerbach has here made a choice that is the starting point for his entire position.

Third, his failure to recognize that there is bound to be a human element in any basic starting point a person chooses. For if it is human wishes, dependence, longings, and strivings that determine our response to our existence in the world, then "every claim by a human mind is invalidated. The logical end of this path is complete skepticism …"[16]

The obvious question to be asked, then, is why stop at the existence of God in particular? In the history of thought, scepticism about this has spread further to question ideas of morality and justice, arts and culture, indeed the objectivity of any knowledge at all. In other words, theology is not the only discipline challenged by projectionism, and the responses across the various disciplines have many family resemblances.

On the other hand, those who continue to believe in God should acknowledge that their conceptions of God might to some extent be vulnerable to Feuerbach's criticisms. Even if the idea of God being completely "made up" by man can be critiqued, for the reasons already given in the opening chapter, there can be little doubt that he has often been the subject of a human "makeover". A failure to acknowledge this masks any claim to absolute knowledge of God untainted by human lack of clarity, one-sidedness, or error. Since all of us have a propensity to infuse our understanding of anything or anyone, including God, with some degree of self-interest or self-distortion, one of Feuerbach's most signal contributions is to raise the question of how any genuine knowledge of God is possible.

This will be an ongoing issue for discussion in the remainder of this book, particularly in the concluding chapter.

5

GOD AS A SUBSTITUTE FOR OPPRESSIVE CONDITIONS

Karl Marx

Feuerbach's influence upon his radical contemporaries was considerable. One of those was Karl Marx (1818–83), who openly acknowledged his debt to Feuerbach. Marx wrote personally to Feuerbach of the deep respect and love he held for him.[1] Elsewhere he declared that "there is no other road for truth and freedom for you than the one that leads through *Feuerbach* [the stream of fire]. Feuerbach is the purgatory of the present."[2]

Marx also castigated Christians for failing to publicly admit that an outsider and opponent had shown them the true essence of their faith. So well had Feuerbach done his job that the young Marx confidently stated that "the criticism of religion has been essentially completed, and the criticism of religion is the presupposition of all criticism".[3]

In certain respects, however, Marx later refashioned Feuerbach's view. While his overall position has less influence today than in previous years, his critique of religion has been subsumed into other approaches.

Karl Marx was born into a family that had rabbis on both his mother's and his father's side of the family. In order to practise law, his father nominally converted to Christianity, though his real sympathies lay more with the views of the French Enlightenment. Karl's youthful attitude to religion surfaced in a paper he had to write on a Christian topic in order to graduate from his Lutheran high school. In this quite orthodox essay he wrote:

> *man stands, the only creature who does not fulfil its goal, the only member in all Creation not worthy of the God that created him. But the benevolent Creator does not hate his handiwork; he wanted to elevate it to his own level and He sent us his Son, through whom He calls to us ... In the union with Christ, therefore, we turn, before everything, our loving eye toward God, feel for Him an ardent gratitude, sink joyfully on our knees before Him.*[4]

Marx's interest in religion continued during his early philosophical studies, which at that time incorporated theological concerns. But this did not last long. His doctoral essay on ancient Greek views of nature (1841) celebrated Democritus's liberation of ancient Man from bondage to the gods and declared that the most popular proof of God's existence demonstrated nothing more than what people imagined was the case. Apart from an investigation of the religion of the Jews three years later in *The Jewish Question*, from this point he only discussed religion where it affected economic and political issues.[5] Overall, "Marx's development can be summed up as follows: At first he criticised religion philosophically, then he criticised religion politically, and at last he criticised religion, philosophy and politics, and all other ideologies, economically."[6]

Though his remarks on religion were occasional and unsystematic, in the process he significantly reformulated Feuerbach's critique. In examining his contribution, we should note the idea of God that he had in mind. It was not so much the traditional Christian one but Hegel's reinterpretation of it. This did not portray God as a vital and dynamic personal being in direct and intimate communication with individuals, but as absolute spirit progressing towards self-realization through his involvement in and transformation of the human and material world. This is the God that Marx questioned and rejected.

Marx's contribution to the critique

Though Marx did not have a great deal to say about religion directly, from his writings we can identify a number of ways in which he further developed a critique of it. For Marx, what Feuerbach had demonstrated beyond doubt was that

> *Man makes religion, religion does not make man ... Man, who in his search for a supernatural being in the fantastic reality of heaven found only a reflection of himself, will no longer be able to find only the semblance of his own self, a non human being, where he seeks and must seek his true reality ... indeed, religion is the self-awareness and self-regard of man who has not yet found or has already lost himself again.*[7]

He argued that theologians themselves had partly paved the way for this by declaring that all religions prior to their own were human inventions. This evidenced itself in Christianity's attack on paganism, and then in Protestantism's critique of Catholicism. Proponents of Judaism and Christianity needed to acknowledge that these stages in the evolution of the human spirit should now be left behind. Marx saw Christianity as the sublime fulfilment of Judaism, even if it was so heavenly preoccupied that it was less practically influential.

Like Feuerbach, Marx regarded Luther as the one who prepared the way for a humanistic reinterpretation of religion, including its idea of God.

> *Luther to be sure vanquished the bondage of devotion when he replaced it with the bondage of conviction. He shattered faith in authority while he restored the authority of faith. He transformed parsons into laymen and laymen into parsons. He emancipated the body from its chains while he made religiosity the innerness of man. He freed man from outward religiosity while he put chains on the heart. But while Protestantism was not the true solution it was the true formulation of the problem. It was therefore no longer a struggle of the layman against the parson outside himself, but of a struggle with his own inner parson, his parson nature.*[8]

For these reasons, Marx regarded Protestantism, and its successor, Deism, as the most suitable forms of religion. He also viewed Bayle as the one whose metaphysical scepticism opened the door to full materialism and atheism.

In two respects Marx felt that Feuerbach had not gone far enough. First, he regarded humankind too abstractly in terms of its general essence rather than concretely in terms of its social, economic, and political life. Recognizing this leads to a different account of how religion was invented. It is not the human species that created gods but the actual world of men, the state, and society. The divine world is therefore nothing more than an inversion of the real one. It is we who turn this into a general worldview, make it a way of giving meaning to life, accord it a spiritual quality and significance, regard it as the ultimate moral sanction, and experience it as a basis of consolation. Though this only realizes in fantasy what it is to be human, it would be wrong to evaluate it in purely negative terms. As well as being an expression of our unfulfilled state, in its own way it is a protest against it. In one of Marx's most quoted statements, "Religion is the sigh of the afflicted creature, the soul of a heartless world, as it is also the spirit of spiritless conditions. It is the *opium* of the people."[9] While he never developed this idea in any detail, it does give us a genuine insight into Marx's understanding.

For Marx, then, religion in general, and its idea of God in particular, is not just a narcotic that drugs people into insensibility. It is rather a way of enduring and compensating for the oppressive conditions under which most live. Initially this provided the most effective means for attacking the existing system and offered the most useful way of educating the working class to challenge and change their situation. But now we need to go beyond this. Here Marx agrees with Feuerbach:

> *The abolition of religion as the illusory happiness is the demand for their real happiness. The demand to abandon the illusions about their condition is the demand to give up a condition that requires illusions. Hence criticism of religion is in embryo a criticism of this vale of tears whose halo is religion.*[10]

By the same token Marx believed it was wrong to celebrate the denial of God as the positive antidote to religion, as many previous critics had done.

> *Atheism ... no longer has any meaning, for atheism is a negation of God, and postulates the existence of man through this negation ... but socialism as socialism no longer stands in need of this mediation ... [It] is man's positive self-consciousness, no longer mediated through the annulment of religion.*[11]

Second, for Marx, Feuerbach did not understand that the driving force in projecting human possibilities into the divine sphere lay in a basic social contradiction. A fault line ran through the world in which he lived that affected not only people's inner life and relationships but also their economic and political life. It was not enough to experience individual or interpersonal liberation, or be satisfied with modest improvements in our working and political life. Now that the criticism of religion has been completed, "It is the immediate task of philosophy ... to expose human self-alienation in its *unholy form* after it has been unmasked in its *holy form*. Criticism of heaven is thus transformed into criticism of earth, *criticism of religion* into *criticism of law*, and *criticism of theology* into *criticism of politics*."[12]

It is this criticism that propelled Marx into the large-scale investigation of past and present human societies found in *Capital* (1867). This led him to the conclusion that work was the creative force in human life and that it was the structures of production that most shaped human activity and creativity. For Marx, unlike d'Holbach, humankind was not merely an expression of physical matter but an agent and product of economic activity. His was a dynamic rather than mechanistic, historical rather than natural, materialism. All forms of human culture, including religion, art, law, and politics, were merely a reflection of these basic forces. Only as changes occurred in the latter would changes take place in the former.

Religion had no real independent existence and was merely a symptom of this-worldly realities. According to Marx, earlier types of human association all produced ideas of god and forms of religion through which one group dominated another. The slave-based society of classical times was mirrored in Greek and Roman religion, the serf-based feudal society of the Middle Ages in Catholicism, and the labour-based industrial society of the modern period in Protestantism. Since religion was so determined by socio-economic factors, Marx felt there was little point in attacking or reinterpreting particular theological ideas, even about God. It was more important to analyse the contradictions that underlay oppressive socio-economic conditions and to outline the revolutionary changes required to introduce a more humane and harmonious society: "The criticism of religion ends with the ... categorical imperative to overthrow all conditions in which man is a degraded, enslaved, abandoned, contemptible being."[13]

Christianity was no help here, as its social principles had justified slavery in antiquity, glorified serfdom in the Middle Ages, and celebrated class distinctions in modern times. In fact, throughout its whole history it had honoured submission and self-abasement. Things would only change when the division of labour that alienated working people from their efforts, and the existence of private property that defrauded the poor over against the rich, were overcome. This would usher in the Communist utopia and only then would religion come to an end and the idea of God disappear. Moving toward this, as the best known of his "Theses on

Feuerbach" has it, required thinkers to actively rouse the oppressed classes to directly work for change. Up till now "philosophers [had] only *interpreted* the world in various ways; the point, however, is to *change* it".[14]

Evaluating Marx's approach to religion

It is difficult to ignore the truth in some of what Marx was advocating. For example, anyone with a sense of history or knowledge of current affairs can point to examples of the way religion has often sided with the rich and powerful over against the poor and powerless. Christians should also empathize with the prophetic tone and challenge to commitment contained in some of Marx's writings, such as his "Theses on Feuerbach" and *Communist Manifesto*. A number of his other works have a global dimension and visionary character that is familiar to Christian ears. It is also the case that the disadvantaged in society have sometimes relied wholly on a future heavenly reversal of their unjust conditions rather than seeking to improve them. Down through the centuries, views of God have also been partly influenced by prevailing social and political attitudes. On other counts, however, his treatment of religion in general, and his view of God in particular, raises some serious questions.

1. His view of God

Although Marx extended Feuerbach's analysis of the idea of God, unfortunately he did not discuss in detail how social and economic factors specifically affected its origin and development. It was because he felt doing this was not particularly important that he overlooked it. Whatever we think of this, it does make it harder to judge the persuasiveness of his view of how this idea arose and changed. In one place Marx admits the difficulty of doing this in saying: "It is, in reality, much easier to discover by analysis the earthly core of the misty creations of religions, than, conversely, it is, to develop from the actual relations of life the corresponding celestialised forms of those relations."[15] It is to his credit that he acknowledges this but it tends to leave his view too much in the speculative category.

Realizing this, his friend and frequent collaborator Friedrich Engels (1820–95) devoted more effort to an investigation of various aspects of human origins. However, he made little attempt to connect this with any discussion of how invention of the gods took place. Karl Kautsky (1854–1938), one of Marxism's later leading thinkers, attempted to fill in this gap for the development of Christian ideas of God in his book *The Foundations of Christianity* (1908). He contended that this movement arose out of a proletarian Jewish movement that rose up against the Romans. Only when this failed did it increasingly deflect its hopes onto heavenly beings and realities. This allowed it to become increasingly co-opted by the Roman state.

Kautsky's portrait of Christianity as simply a reflection of these developments does not correlate well with what historians deduce actually happened. Their studies of early Christianity show that it especially attracted people from what we would term middle-class groups. Though reversal of their unjust conditions drew in some from lower status groups as well, it was not mainly made up of these. Both Engels and Kautsky also acknowledge that it possessed a genuine earthly as well as heavenly orientation – an interest in life in the world as well as their life with God.

The Marxist who most filled out how the idea of God developed in biblical times was the philosopher Ernst Bloch. He did this especially in his major work entitled *Atheism in Christianity* (1972). His framework for this came from his studies of a radical Protestant reformer, named Thomas Muntzer, whom he saw as a "Theologian of Revolution" (1921). He focused especially on how views of the Messiah and of the "end times" affected the developing understanding of God. Bloch argued that while God was initially as "God-above" all that happens, after the Exodus this idea of God was itself transcended by one of "God-becoming" what the future unfolded. In Christianity, this metamorphosed into a belief in "God-immanent" in Jesus. This laid the basis for ultimately reinterpreting God in humanistic terms, specifically how people could discover possibilities not yet envisioned.

Bloch's interpretation, which is both imaginative and sophisticated, rightly affirms the biblical view of God as transcendent, history-making, and immanent. The real difficulty is that in the biblical writings, God is all these things all the time, not in the gradual way he proposes. It is only that developmental schema that allows him to argue for an increasingly humanistic trajectory in the Jewish–Christian view of God.

2. His view of socio-economic influence

More substantial investigations into the relationship between religious and social and economic factors – some undertaken by historians without any express religious commitment – provide a different picture from Marx's hints about the relationship between social and economic factors and religious ideas and practices developed. This is an area that always troubled me when reading Marx, partly because some of my own work, and the work of others around me, increasingly highlighted the innovations Christianity introduced into the world of its day and the difference it increasingly made in the following centuries. Whereas Greeks and Romans essentially had a cyclical view of social and political life, Christianity insisted that God's involvement in people's lives led first to personal and then, over time, to wider social and political reform.[16] Such innovations as the founding of hospitals for the sick stemmed directly from their view of God as vitally compassionate and caring. The belief that God's image was present in all people, whatever their status or gender, led to the elimination of slavery in Europe within a few centuries and to an increased respect for and appreciation of the role of women in family and wider life.

More generally, the radical nature of this new faith led to a significant transformation of the whole classical outlook on life. A recent well-known historian points particularly to

> ... *the liberation it offered from fatalism, cosmic despair, and the terror of occult agencies; the immense dignity it conferred upon the human person; its subversion of the cruelest aspects of pagan society; its ... partial demystification of political power; its ability to create moral community ... and its elevation of charity above all other virtues ... [therefore] ... it can be called in the fullest sense a "revolution" ... so vast in its consequences as actually to have created a new conception of the world, of history, of human nature, of time, and of the moral good.*[17]

Later, during the Middle Ages and Reformation, the emphasis on knowledge in Christian belief and experience, especially of God and his purposes in the world, led to an increasing interest in education, culminating in the birth of universities for the study of law, philosophy, and theology. The conviction that God's creation was characterized by orderliness also laid the foundations for the development of modern science.[18] From the seventh century onwards, a further significant discovery took place in independent churches in England. As ordinary members learned that God's presence and gifting among them enabled them to govern their own affairs rather than be subservient to a clerical hierarchy, they began to realize that they could govern their wider social and political affairs. This was one of the major catalysts in the move towards more democratic forms of government.

These are just a few examples of ways in which the Christian view of God, and worldview, offered not only spiritual consolation in the face of injustice and oppression, but brought about substantial social, economic, and political change. What is the upshot of all this? Even if we combine what Marx and those influenced by him adduce about the role of social and economic factors in generating and modifying views of God, much is still left incomplete. We still do not get a sufficiently well-based or comprehensive account of how one explains, indeed can be reduced to, the other.

3. His view of Man

Since, for Marx, it is ultimately humankind, in and through the social and economic forces confronting them, that is the source of ideas about God and religion, it is necessary to look briefly at his understanding of human nature. Serious questions surround Marx's view of human nature, although he does provide a more concrete understanding of this than Feuerbach, that is earthed in people's everyday work and relationships. This is one of Marx's most significant contributions. It means that when he talks about the life and world of ordinary people it is much more recognizable.

Yet Marx's view of what it is to be human also has its limitations. First, it does not take the long-standing human tendency towards self-centredness, and on occasions outright evil, seriously enough. Indeed, "Marx underestimated the power of evil and the destiny of death. Like Ludwig Feuerbach he denied evil and ignored death."[19]

Even if we accept Marx's view that a change in socio-economic conditions will alter this, experience would seem to suggest that there is something endemic in human beings that continues to prevent them from fulfilling their potential. This has been borne out in practical attempts by a variety of Communist regimes to put Marx's views into practice, however much other factors may have also contributed to their failure.

It is not that Marx fails to identify a profound contradiction in human nature. At the root of this problem is a highly questionable bifurcation of human nature. He rightly recognizes a gap between the contribution made by ordinary people through their work and the benefits they receive from it. For him this lies at the root of their basic feeling of alienation. He goes on to objectify this division of the self into a division between worker and employer, labour and capital. Freedom from servitude only comes with the final victory of oppressed workers, the proletariat over their despotic masters. The question is, does this analysis of the human problem go deep enough?

Others would argue, and not only on religious grounds, that the problem lies deeper: within and not just between human beings. It lies in the division between what they would like to be and what they are, in their aspirations as persons more than as workers, and in their inability to attain this because something within them works against their best interests. In other words, there is an inner flaw that runs right through them. This is what is biblically defined as sin. It is Marx's failure to recognize this that prevents him from seeing the possibility that God exists in the first place. For combined with this flaw is sometimes the belief that, if anything can overcome it, it is only by human invention and effort that this can take place. If this is the case, there is no need to look for assistance and empowerment from a God in confronting and at least partly overcoming these destructive human forces.

Marx's ambivalent legacy

On the one hand Marx presents his approach as highly empirical. He advances it as having history demonstrably on its side and views it as a purely scientific exercise. This opens up the wider issue of how much it possesses a quasi-religious character. If so, it raises the possibility that in denying the reality of God something else may be deified in God's place. According to the social philosopher Robert Tucker:

> The religious essence of Marxism is superficially obscured by Marx's rejection of the traditional religions. This took the form of a repudiation of "religion" as such and an espousal of "atheism". Marx's atheism, however, meant only a denial of the transmundane character of the God of traditional Western religion. It did not mean the

> *denial of a supreme being. [Indeed] denial of the*
> *transmundane God was only a negative way of*
> *asserting that "man" should be regarded as the*
> *supreme being .... Thus his atheism was a positive*
> *religious proposition.*[20]

Tucker goes on to point out that structurally Marxism itself invites analysis as a religious system – indeed, that it is influenced by the universal religions with their idea of one God that preceded it, especially Christianity.

- Like Christianity, it offers a comprehensive vision of the whole of reality, an integrated, all-inclusive understanding of everything that exists, a frame of reference within which all the basic questions of life are answered.

- Like Christianity, it views human life in the context of natural order and historical development, in providing an account of reality that has a beginning, middle and end, with its own Communist version of paradise-lost, paradise-sought and paradise-regained.

- Like Christianity, it has a central theme that revolves around human regeneration, a movement from enslavement to freedom, a story of radical personal and social transformation.

- Like Christianity, it is based on a unity of theory and practice, worldview and life commitment, reflection and action, and on taking part in an overarching historical and cosmic drama involving all that exists.

This means that Marx's view of religion, however much in it is presented as empirical and scientific, is no more objective than the religious view of life it seeks to replace. But even if it fails as a theory of how belief in God originated and developed, it does suggest how those religions were vulnerable to human makeover in ways that betrayed their true character. As Alasdair MacIntyre says:

> *Religion is only disposed of by the Marxist critique if it is true that the essential characteristic of religion is its other-worldliness, its essential claim to explain phenomena, and its essential function to compensate for human powerlessness and to mask human exploitation ... It must be granted that the Marxist critique of religion holds true for a great deal of religion, and in particular to a great deal of nineteenth century religion.*[21]

We shall return to this challenge in the final chapter.

6

GOD AS A PROJECTION OF REPRESSED DESIRES

Sigmund Freud

Sigmund Freud (1856–1939) was the next major advocate of the view that we created God. In doing so, he pioneered the psychological version of the critique that in fits and starts has developed since his time and continues to this day.

Freud was Jewish by birth and upbringing, though not by conviction. Despite this, he experienced anti-Semitism at various points during his life, particularly in his later years. The form of religion with which he mostly came in contact was the highly formal, liturgical, and hierarchical Catholicism of his homeland, Austria.

He was educated in Vienna, initially studying under a professor of zoology influenced by Charles Darwin. After a time he switched to medicine, in which he received his doctorate in 1881. A few years later he travelled to Paris to study with the founders of abnormal psychology, and there he began to develop his own approach to treating neurotic disorders. On his return to Vienna he started a practice in neurology, out of which developed his interest in psychoanalysis. Later he was appointed Professor of Neurology at the University of Vienna, a position he held until Hitler's occupation of Austria in 1938 forced him to take refuge in England, where he died a year later.

Freud's analysis of religion

According to Freud's own account, he gave up believing in God in his youth. This was most probably around the time he began to react against his father's authority. In the process he came to think of God as a childish creation. Several of his earliest writings foreshadowed his more extensive later treatments of religion. Though appreciative of earlier critiques like Feuerbach's, he felt these lacked an adequate psychological basis.

> *A great part of the mythological view of the world, which reaches far into the most modern religions, is nothing other than psychological processes projected into the outer world. The obscure apprehending of the psychical factors and relationships of the unconscious is mirrored – one has to use here the language of paranoia – in the construction of a super sensible reality which science has to retranslate into the psychology of the unconscious. One could venture in this matter to resolve the myth of paradise, the fall of man, of God, of good and evil, of immortality, and so on, thus transforming metaphysics into metapsychology.*[1]

At the heart of his approach to religion lay the pivotal relationship between the child and the father. "Psychoanalysis has shown us that a personal God is, psychologically, nothing other than an exalted father ... and it brings evidence every day of how young people lose their religious beliefs as soon as their father's authority breaks down."[2] He recounts that at an early stage in his thinking the biblical statement that "God created man in his own image" came to mind and how he mentally reversed this to "man created God in his".[3]

Freud's views on the emergence of religion drew partly on investigations of human origins by Charles Darwin and of ancient myths by James Frazer (1854–1941). Building on their insights he put forward the following scenario. In primeval times, he speculated, people venerated their ancestors without any religious overtones. However, as people began to group together in small hordes, the need arose for a head of the tribe to take care of them. This happened as an older male rose to prominence in each horde, subjected the younger men and appropriated the women. In due course the sons retaliated against their tribal father, killing and consuming him. Overcome by guilt, the new brother clan began to represent the departed father by a sacred totem. They also instituted an annual feast to commemorate the event and it was this that gave birth to religion, as well as to morality, law, and social organization. Since none of the sons were able to become the father's equal, this led them to conceive a tribal god in the form of an imaginary father instead of the material totem.

Freud saw a parallel in this whole development to the growth of an infant into an adult. A child metaphorically "kills off" the natural father when he or she separates from him. An ambiguous love-hate relationship with the father then develops. This amounts to the so-called Oedipus complex. Even when children become adult, infantile attitudes remain and they feel the need for protection.

This led to the birth of a variety of tribal gods. Underlying Freud's psychological reconstruction was a nineteenth-century evolutionary view of progress from mythological, through religious, to scientific understanding. Myth and religion continued to survive only in superstition and in the foundations of language and philosophy.

Freud investigated the move from polytheism to belief in one God in his major work, *Moses and Monotheism* (1939). This development first took place in imperial fourteenth-century BC Egypt when Akhenaton's religious reforms led to a single sun god replacing the long-term practice of polytheism. Freud suggested that Moses was not a Jew but an Egyptian involved in these reforms. After a popular reaction against these upon the Pharaoh's death, Moses decided to found a nation that would remain faithful to monotheistic worship. In the process he humanized Akhenaton's God, though his accompanying rejection of images ensured this God was viewed in spiritual rather than sensual terms. This reawakened views "that had long ago faded from the conscious memory of mankind".[4]

Speculating further, Freud proposed that the Israelites had turned against Moses and killed him. It was a later leader who was confused with Moses who initiated a modified monotheism that prized one God among, rather than instead of, others. This was the volcanic, brooding, arbitrary, and vengeful deity of the earliest writings in the Old Testament.

It was not until the arrival of the major prophets of the Bible that Moses' more profound universal monotheism resurfaced. Here was an all-loving, all-powerful God concerned with truth and justice rather than with ceremony and magic. Later still, unconscious guilt at Moses' death gave rise to the hope of a second Moses. In the following centuries this linked up with a growing sense of discomfort and misfortune among both Jews and non-Jews. This ultimately found its spokesman in the apostle Paul, who declared that "it is because we killed God the Father that we are so unhappy".[5]

This led to his interpretation of Jesus' death as the overdue atonement on the part of one of the nation's brothers for the implicit slaying of their primal father. For those who embraced this, there was a tremendous sense of release. In effect what happened was the installation of a religion of the Son in the place of one based on the Father.

A spiritual regression took place in early Christianity with the development of Mary into a mother goddess and the saints into minor deities. In later Catholicism, other superstitious, magical, and mystical elements reasserted themselves. For Freud, the rise of Islam was a repetition of earlier Jewish tendencies, though less profound because there was no slaying of its founder. Eastern religions, despite their stronger rationalistic tendency, had more in common with pre-religious ancestor cults. While religious beliefs were essentially unreal, they still contained an element of truth. So, for example, monotheism retained the primal memory of a tribal father, even though its idea of a universal godlike one is distorted.

After his studies in the natural sciences, medicine, and psychoanalysis, Freud provided his most systematic and comprehensive account of religion in *The Future of an Illusion* (1927). He approached this as an exercise in cultural reflection rather than as a summary of his small number of clinical studies on the subject. In this he defines religion as comprising "dogmas, assertions about facts and conditions of external (or internal) reality, which tell one something that one has not oneself discovered and which claim that one should give them credence".[6]

Freud goes beyond Feuerbach in two respects. First, such beliefs are not just the expression of people's wishes and fears, but also a compensation for the vagaries of life and social constraints they have suffered. Unlike Feuerbach, more than simply a *direct* projection of what people desire there is an imaginary extension of their deepest hopes. This is the psychological mechanism of *reverse* projection that turns our present conditions on their head. This provides a more persuasive account at the level of motivation. Second, Freud posits that individual religious beliefs cannot simply be seen as a common human *experience* as they are developed from a shared unconscious *inheritance*. The primal father image that gives shape to them is imprinted on the human mind, on which the individual builds their own personal father image.

Unfortunately, says Freud, these attempts at resolving our longings, anxieties, and questions to gain control over our lives are founded on second-hand beliefs rather than first-hand self-authenticating experience. They are not, as some earlier critics asserted, manipulative attempts at deceiving others but rather self-deception through which we hide truth from ourselves. Since they are not based on observation and reasoning, they are nothing more than "illusions, fulfilments of the oldest, strongest and most urgent wishes of mankind".[7]

The difference between illusions and delusions is that while both are derived from wishes, quite apart from the more complicated structure of the latter, "In the case of delusions, we emphasise as essential their being in contradiction with reality. Illusions need not necessarily be false – that is to say, unrealizable or in conflict with reality." [8]

This means that the judgment a person makes about the truth or otherwise of such a belief will depend on their personal attitude. Instead of simply condemning religious beliefs as an illusion, Freud states that mostly we cannot judge their reality value. They can be neither proved nor refuted. But while "it would be very nice if there were a god, who was both creator of the world and a benevolent Providence, if there were a moral order and an after-life … but it is a very striking fact that this is exactly as we are bound to wish it to be".[9]

At this point Freud identifies the one new feature in his approach. Although, as a neutral scientific method, psychoanalysis cannot determine the truth value of a religion, he believes that it strengthens the case against it. He is quite willing to admit that religion has performed great services for human culture, particularly in restraining some of mankind's baser instincts and in helping to develop civilization. But it has failed to make the bulk of people more moral, sociable, and happy. It is now time to distinguish the important historical memories religion enshrines from its illusory wish fulfilments.

In his follow-up work, *Civilisation and its Discontents* (1930), Freud asks where the religious approach to life stands in relation to people's substitute satisfactions for it. Some forgo the quest and instead seek to satisfy their every need. Others withdraw from reality through isolating or intoxicating themselves, or attempt to physically, rationally or mystically control their instincts. It is more effective to sublimate these by working in a professional way, engaging in some artistic or scientific endeavour or, best of all, living a life devoted to loving relationships. On the other hand, a purely aesthetic approach to life loosens the connection with reality and, taken to extremes, leads to paranoia. Whenever this occurs on a mass scale, there is religion. Here Freud goes beyond his more cautious remarks in *The Future of an Illusion*, asserting: "The religions of mankind must be classed among the mass-delusions of this kind."[10]

Though this fixes people in a state of psychic infantilism, its advantage is that it sometimes succeeds in sparing them the onset of an individual neurosis.

Evaluating Freud's approach to religion

For all its negative character, a number of Jewish and Christian thinkers and psychologists find some positive elements in Freud's approach to religion. There is also much to support his view that many, especially popular or deviant, forms of religion are significantly influenced by unconscious wishes, fears, and drives. As we shall see in the concluding chapter, Freud's insights here can help us discern how and where this happens, even in the beliefs of more thoughtful and committed believers.

It is too easy to be put off by his critical approach, especially by his view that God is an imaginary man-made creation of an illusory, even delusory, kind. Certainly many people have discerned a connection between their relationship with their father, or lack of it, and their relationship with God. Sometimes experience of an over-dominant father correlates with an authoritarian view of God. Sometimes a positive experience of a father correlates with a strong God relationship. Sometimes the emotional distance of a father correlates with a lack of intimacy with God. Sometimes the absence of a father correlates with a sense of God's non-existence. In this general connection, one of Freud's followers, Erik Erikson (1902–94), produced a study of Luther examining links between the reformer's relationship with his father and his changing ideas of God.

What do we make of Freud's views more generally?

1. His view of God

While for many Freud rightly stresses the primal and guilt-based nature of the origins of gods, his reconstruction of the way this developed has come under consistent fire in anthropological circles. For example, totemism is nowhere to be found in the beginnings of religion; taboo is a less concrete phenomenon than he adduced; only a few tribes celebrate the killing and eating of a god. Freud's attitude to the growing evidence against his account, some of which was available to him in his lifetime, is revealing. He continued to defend his theory because it tied in with his psychoanalytic findings in a way that other approaches did not. For all Freud's belief in scientific enquiry and evidence as the touchstone of truth and antidote to religion, in this area he did not remain faithful to his basic convictions.

Although there have been some recent attempts to build on Freud's views of the Jewish understanding of God, his account is also at odds with historical investigations during and after his time. There is no basis for the view that Moses was a high-ranking Egyptian or that he died the way Freud posited. There is no link between the monotheisms of Akhenaton IV and Moses, and no evidence for the existence of a second Midianite Moses-like figure. While Israel's view of God developed over time, especially through the prophets, its depiction of God's uniqueness and character were already present in Moses' time.

As far as Christianity is concerned, his view that Christ was a mythical rather than actual figure has no support from classical historians, who regard his life, his work as a religious teacher, and his death at the hands of the Romans, as undeniable historical fact. While these anthropological and historical inadequacies call into question Freud's particular account of religious origins, they do not refute his general theory of wish-fulfilment and guilt displacement underlying it.

2. His view of religious experience

What then of Freud's interpretation of religious experience? Freud later admitted that his analysis of religion in *The Future of an Illusion* was concerned "much less with the deepest sources of religious feeling than with what the ordinary man understands by his religion".[11]

For this reason various critics of Freud rightly call into question the limited, essentially shallow, *range* of religious experience he discussed. He was influenced here by the mixture of popular devotional and highly ceremonial elements in the Viennese Catholicism of his day that was refracted through the experience of his mentally disturbed patients. This was marked by a sentimental and anxious view of God, as well as an overly formal and obsessive approach to religious practices.

The *character* of religious experience also comes in for one-sided analysis by Freud. He believed that the very nature of religious beliefs meant that they could not be questioned or debated. This is very different from frequent biblical appeals by God to "come let us reason together" and Paul's insistence that believers "test everything".[12] For William Meissner (d. 2010), who was influenced by Freud but attempted to remedy defects in his account, Freud's analysis of emphasis upon religious development being mainly a more intense repetition of its origins is inadequate to explain the dynamism of religious experience. Meissner himself offers the first comprehensive psychological analysis of this. He portrays it as passing from an initial narcissism, through conscious dependence, to genuine faith.[13] In addition, as the psychologist Gordon Allport (1897–1967) says of the religious dimension of life, "it is impossible for this sentiment in a mature stage of development to remain disconnected from the mainstream of experience, relegated to a corner of the fantasy life where it provides an escape clause in one's contact from reality".[14]

Interestingly, Freud himself detected what he called "a religion of a sublimated kind" in his friend and disciple, the Swiss pastor Oscar Pfister (1873–1956).[15] In one place, he even entertains the possibility that religion will never disappear and so comes close to a functional view of its value. In another, though he never attempted to explore it, he acknowledged that behind the feeling of infantile helplessness might lie something deeper.

Influenced by Freud, and based on a wide range of clinical case studies, Ana-Maria Rizzuto does explore this in her study *The Birth of the Living God* (1979).[16] For her, belief in God should not be regarded either as an hallucination or as the result of repression. Human beings, she says, cannot live without relating to some idea of God. Just as children need people and toys to transition from childhood to adulthood, we also need belief in a cosmic object to do this. This generally becomes most appealing and powerful at the moment of parental – not just paternal – conflict. In time this image of God is amplified and modified by the influence of other authority figures and role models such as teachers and religious leaders. Like a work of art or musical composition, each person's image of God is an individual creation. Most recently, Rizzuto has produced a psychoanalytic analysis of how and why Freud himself came to reject God from his earliest years.[17]

3. His view of the psychological processes involved

How far have the key psychological components of Freud's view that God is an imaginary human construct been confirmed by later experimental research?[18]

First, there is the question of how well based Freud's theory is about the role of the Oedipus complex in familial relations. While cumulative psychological and anthropological studies confirm its existence, they do not accord it the central place or universal significance Freud gave to it. As already mentioned, Rizzuto has demonstrated that religious influence of children involves both parents, indeed most strongly the opposite sex parent. Also that positive qualities parents model appear to be more influential than negative ones.[19] A range of experimental studies has also demonstrated the process of the *repression* of unwelcome realities into consciousness. Though these findings are not related to the religious consequences of this, and they do not prove this cornerstone of Freud's critique of God, they do leave it open. Other studies have explored and confirmed the role of *projection* in transferring hidden personality traits to others, but some of their methods have come under criticism and so far there is scarcely any investigation of its role in religion.

Since projection is so central to Freud's approach to religion, it deserves a closer look. Freud distinguished between its "abnormal" and "normal" occurrence. In everyday life we often clothe others with our own unconscious behaviours and the external world with our own inner perceptions. For Freud, as long as we are conscious of what we are doing, this is quite defensible. Unfortunately little attempt has been made to explore whether this normal, everyday use could be extended to its presence in the experience of God.

One attempt to do this, by Fokke Sierksma (1917–77), focuses on non-cognitive Buddhist approaches to the divine rather than the more personal God of the main monotheistic religions.[20] Others in the field of projective psychology do not engage in much discussion of its role in religion at all.[21] So far, then, this whole component in Freud's account remains without empirical foundation.

4. His logical validity

Many critics have accused Freud of committing the *genetic fallacy* – that is, of assuming that an explanation of what gives rise to an experience explains the experience itself. As Gordon Allport says, "Origins can tell us nothing about the validity of a belief. Neither can origins characterise the nature of the belief as it now exists, nor explain its part in the present economy of a life."[22]

The reason for this is that we can come to believe something true on false rational or emotional grounds. It might only be later that we find better reasons for doing so. Freud often speaks as if he is unaware of this crucial distinction. This is relevant to what he has to say about the role of wish-fulfilment in the area of belief in God. As we saw in drawing on C. S. Lewis earlier, the desire that something be true is irrelevant to whether it really is or not. The desire for God to exist would only count against his actual existence if there was conclusive evidence to the contrary. In general, the presence of natural factors in religious experience does not logically rule out the possibility of a God who created, sustains, and works through such factors.

A related fallacy that Freud lies open to being accused of is confusion of the *content* of something and what it *signifies*. Let us agree, for example, that the formation of a child's image of God is initially derived from the child's relationship with their father. It could be argued that since we can only absorb and interpret new experiences by assimilating them to previous ones, with respect to God the child-father relationship is the most obvious candidate. We could argue further that the religious significance of this relationship is a product of the way God designed the universe. Instead of speaking about deifying parents and projecting them onto some supernatural reality, there is then a divine arrangement through which God is able to reveal himself to children. If this were the case, psychological processes would only account for the particular texture, not substance, of people's religious experience.

Freud also fell prey to the error of *guilt by association*. Simply because two phenomena sometimes appear together does not mean they are psychologically identical. Consider here Freud's frequent coupling of religion with neurosis. Though in places he states that the link between these is one of analogy rather than identity, he tends to describe religion as a pathological affair. While religion does appear more often in neurosis than other aspects of life, such as science, it does so because it brings our passions more strongly into play. The majority of people with religious convictions do not practise these in any pathological way. To take another example, the greater frequency of a persecution mania in delusions has not led people to conclude that our human instinct for self-preservation is pathological.

Freud's ambiguous legacy

Freud based such hopes as he had for mankind on science. He held that reason alone, as embodied in science, was objective, self-correcting, and well founded. But in his writings this conviction all too easily slips into a kind of fundamentalist scientism. This shows up in his positivist evolutionary belief in the three stages of humankind – mythic, religious, and scientific.

Although he felt that religion did not meet this test, Freud did occasionally ascribe his view of it to his personal beliefs rather than scientific reason. In a letter to his friend Oscar Pfister he admitted that the whole of *The Future of an Illusion* was written on this basis.[23] Yet it is often precisely in such contexts that he asserts that the practice of psychoanalysis necessarily involves the abandonment of religion: "Freud's customary detachment fails him here. Confronting religion, psychoanalysis shows itself to be what it is: the last great formulation of nineteenth century secularism."[24]

What Freud in fact demonstrates is a kind of religious belief in science, or in psychoanalysis, as a kind of alternative religion. For as Antoine Vergote shows in his comprehensive study of Freud's attempts at analysing the roots and nature of religion, "The validity of religious belief can neither be substantiated nor refuted by scientific reasoning."[25]

Interestingly, at the personal level Freud's scientistic tendency was not always apparent. As his daughter Anna Freud points out, his letters reflect a more open approach to religion, for, unlike in his published works, scattered through these are phrases like "with God's help", "if God so wills", and "into the keeping of the Lord"; others such as "God's grace", "God above", "the good Lord"; and still others like "my secret prayer", "in the next world", and "if someday we meet above".[26] However conventional, rhetorical or audience-specific these may have been, it is hard to dismiss them as mere figures of speech, especially in one who believed that slips of the tongue were important psychological indicators. All this suggests that there are other elements in Freud's approach that provide the basis for a more positive view of God and religion.

7

God as the Symbol of Human Potential

Erich Fromm

As we have seen, Marx sought to ground Feuerbach's inversion of God and humankind in the concrete world of everyday work and production. For his part, Freud sought to ground it more deeply in our personal and collective psyche. Both were seeking to make what they regarded as still too abstract a critique more down to earth and life changing. But so long as these two approaches were presented as alternatives, they were incomplete. Those who became their followers mostly operated within one framework or the other. What was needed was someone to try and bring the two approaches together. It was left to Erich Fromm to attempt this as part of a wider project of applying psychological ideas to an analysis of social realities. Though influenced by Freud, Fromm criticized his mentor's early view of human drives as a tension between desire and repression, as well as his inability to move beyond patriarchal attitudes reflective of early twentieth-century Vienna.

Born in 1900, Fromm was the son of orthodox Jewish parents, with three generations of rabbis in his family line. He first studied sociology and then trained in psychoanalysis. After Hitler came to power, he left Germany for Switzerland and then America, with a fifteen-year interval in Mexico before retiring back to first the United States and then finally Switzerland, where he died in 1980.

As a young man Fromm's study of the Talmud helped shape his worldview, but then in his mid-twenties he began to explore secular interpretations of scriptural ideas. This led him to recast the Adam and Eve story, so that eating from the Tree of Life signified the start of humankind's ability to act independently rather than disobediently towards God. It developed their capacity to distinguish between good and evil and to discover their own moral values rather than those imposed on them by an authoritarian God.

After a time he joined the Frankfurt School for Social Research, which was endeavouring to integrate Freudian and Marxian viewpoints. Ultimately, however, he modified this in a more humanistic direction. A prolific writer, his works cover a wide range of topics, including acquisitiveness, freedom, aggression, love, and authoritarianism. Those that most extensively address the issue of religion are *Escape from Freedom* (1941), *Psychoanalysis and Religion* (1950), *The Dogma of Christ* (1963), *You Shall Be as Gods* (1966), and to a lesser extent *Man for Himself* (1948) and *The Art of Loving* (1957). Along with two co-authors he wrote *Zen Buddhism and Psychoanalysis* (1960), exploring the relationship between the two.

Fromm's integrative analysis of religion

Fromm's interpretation of how the idea of God arose is based on his general understanding of the origins of religion. He begins by defining religion in broader terms than the major world faiths. It encompasses "any system of thought and action shared by a group which gives the individual a frame of orientation and a sense of devotion".[1]

For him, religious need is deeply rooted in human existence. Though people originally lived in harmony with themselves, others, and nature, a split developed between these as they started to exercise self-consciousness, reason, and imagination. Religion arises from this division.

Along with its ethical dimension, religion springs from:

- a sense of wonder at the fact of one's existence;

- an ultimate concern with self-meaning and realization;

- the experience of unity with oneself, others, and nature.

In defence of this view of religion, he cites Freud's suggestion that Communism could be regarded as a secular religion. Where does the notion of God that is found in major theistic religions fit into this definition? For Fromm, "God" is part of the picture but he prefers to avoid understanding the term literally. Two things follow from this broad definition: no person or culture, past or present, has been without religious need or religion itself; "the question is not *religion or not* but *which kind of religion*, whether it is one furthering man's development, the unfolding of his specifically human powers, or one paralysing them".[2]

This is a different attitude from that characteristic of Marx and Freud, even Feuerbach, though it has more in common with the latter in taking religion itself seriously and means that anyone who seriously analyses religion must attend not only to its psychological or sociological roots but to the issue of its value and validity.

Fromm begins his analysis of religion, and the varying approaches to the divine within it, by distinguishing between earlier primitive and later advanced types. Animism develops via polytheism into monotheism, and this develops from a matriarchal into a patriarchal form. Below the surface of modern societies, various kinds of individualized primitive religion continue to thrive alongside the higher transcendent religions.

Fromm then introduces a further basic distinction that cuts across theistic and non-theistic religions, traditional religions and philosophical systems, and even particular religious traditions. *Authoritarian* religion emphasizes external control and dutiful obedience, with moral criteria and awareness occupying only a secondary place. *Humanistic* religion emphasizes personal potential and growth on the basis of conscious moral norms and principles. He regards Protestantism as an example of the former; Isaiah, Jesus, and mysticism of the latter. What distinguishes these is the presence of powerlessness versus strength, unthinking compliance versus self-realization, propositional assent versus experiential conviction.

Fromm focuses next on the dynamics of these two approaches to religion. It is here that the idea of humankind creating God in its own image comes into play.

> *While in humanistic religion God is the image of man's higher self, a symbol of what man potentially is or ought to become, in authoritarian religion God becomes the sole possessor of what was originally man's; of his reason and his love. In the latter man projects the best he has on to God and thus impoverishes himself ... the mechanism of projection is the very same which can be observed in interpersonal relationships of a masochistic, submissive character.[3]*

As a result, humankind's powers become alienated, as the only access now to what is intrinsically human is indirectly through God. The more slavishly we depend on God, the less faith we have both in ourselves and in others. The more we give ourselves to God, the less of ourselves there is to offer. The more we project ourselves upwards into God, the less our humanity actually becomes, for the conditions that lead to authoritarian and humanistic religion do not only lie within. People's character "is moulded by the total configuration of their practice of life – more precisely, by the sociological and political structure of their society".[4]

In saying this, Fromm frees Freud's emphasis on the Father complex from its narrow sexual focus and views it in a broader social way.

We turn next to Fromm's interpretation of key beliefs in Judaism and Christianity.

1. The idea of God emerged out of a socio-political structure in which tribal leaders possessed a monopoly on power. This led to the group conceptualizing its supreme value by means of an analogy with the chief power in society. Originally "God was only an idealised man, perhaps not too different from the Olympian gods of the Greeks – a God who

resembles man in his virtues and in his vices, who can be challenged by men".[5]

In the Old Testament the idea develops in a way that corresponds to the experience of the Jewish nation. In the first stage, God is visualized as an absolute ruler, though this is counterbalanced by the idea that humankind, represented by Adam, could become divine and therefore potentially God's rival. However, as already noted, people's original challenge to God should not be regarded as sin but as the start of human history and they are only punished so that God may remain supreme. As human beings begin a life independent of God, human history gets under way. In the second stage, God establishes a covenant with Noah and his descendants that guarantees humans and animals the right to life. In doing this God becomes less an absolute ruler than a kind of constitutional monarch. This general covenant with humanity is followed by a more specific covenant between God and the Hebrews that gives rise to the Jewish nation.

For Fromm, the struggle against the making of visible representations of the divine (idolatry) is one of the principal themes in the Old Testament. The idol represents a backward step into the craving for material instead of spiritual things and for manipulative instead of enabling power. Over against this development, especially in the nations around Israel, the earlier Jewish understanding of God developed in two main directions.

First, while the prophets talked about the fact that God *is* and God *acts*, there are no speculations about his *essence* or *character*. Initially this led to post-biblical Judaism emphasizing even more strongly the importance of imitating God's actions rather than knowing him intimately. This is why in the Talmud there is no theology, let alone orthodoxy, but instead theopraxy and orthopraxy – that is, godly and right practices. Maimonides' rejection altogether of positive attributes to describe God is the culmination of this development. For Fromm, this way of thinking "leads – in its ultimate consequence – though not one contemplated by Maimonides – to the end of theology",[6] that is, to the need to talk about God at all.

Second, both biblical and later Jewish thought demonstrated a preference for this "negative theology" by their insistence that affirming God basically meant rejecting idols. In the prophets, God's uniqueness does not lie in his unity over against their plurality, but in what he is not – not man, not an artefact, not an institution, not the state, not nature. Imitating God is primarily a refusal to transfer human qualities to an idol and submitting to an alienated and impoverished experience of self. This is why "fear of, and submission to, God diminishes more and more as the concept of God develops in the course of the later tradition. Man becomes God's partner, almost his equal."[7]

In this way Fromm prepares the ground for developing a religious attitude focused more on human beings and their potential rather than on God and his claims.

Since the prohibiting of idols is raised to as high a place as acknowledging God, if not higher, mankind does not really need to worship God at all. All it requires is to avoid blaspheming God or venerating false images of him. This involves directing our religious capacities in fully ethical and humanistic ways. In doing this "we move from the level of theology to that of psychology, and especially psychoanalysis",[8] though one that must enlarge its essential framework beyond that provided by Freud.

2. Fromm's book on early Christian views of the deity of Christ dates from a time when he was more strictly Freudian, and was written in reaction to a paper by Theodor Reik (1888–1969) from a more fully orthodox Freudian point of view. Whatever changes his views later underwent, Fromm deemed the book sufficiently compatible with his more developed views to republish it later in life. Unlike Reik's stress on the unchanging psychological state of individuals and groups in the centuries after Christ, Fromm begins by arguing that in the time of Christ there were

> ... *different groups with different social and psychic*
> *interests and the victory of dogma is not the result*
> *of an inner psychic conflict analogous to that in the*
> *individual, but is the result, rather, of an historical*
> *development which, in consequence of quite different*
> *external circumstances ... leads to the victory of one*
> *movement and defeat of another.*[9]

Unlike the dominant religious groups of his day, the Sadducees and Pharisees, Christ represented the disadvantaged rather than middle and upper classes. His message of the coming kingdom of God allowed them to project into future fantasy what had been presently denied them. They identified with him not only as a man articulating their longings and protest, but also as one who becomes God. This, says Fromm, echoing Freud, gave voice to their unconscious desire to replace the primal Father. Developing views of Christ's crucifixion later enabled them to displace their death wishes against the Father to the Son through the former's death in the latter.

In the next two centuries, Christians began to infiltrate the middle class and increasingly became the religion of large circles of the ruling class. Increasingly, leading apologists and theologians gave Christ a higher status in the Godhead. By the time of Constantine's proclamation in favour of Christianity (AD 313), the move from a slave-based to a feudal state was reflected in formulating the belief that Christ had always possessed divine status. From then on, not even in fantasy could the disaffected classes entertain hope for social and material transformation. Consequently:

> ... *the fantasy satisfaction became different. The masses no longer identified with the Son in order to dethrone the Father in fantasy ... but, rather, in order to enjoy his love and grace. People no longer expected an imminent historical change, but believed, rather, that deliverance had already taken place ... This is the core meaning contained in the logical contradiction of the dogma of the Trinity.*[10]

Simultaneously, argues Fromm, their aggressive impulses were turned inwards so that they identified with the suffering Christ and increasingly looked for consolation from his mother Mary and from the institutional church. This perpetuation of the infantile state, self-annihilation of the Son, and the continued dominance of the Father, was the psychic attitude corresponding to the place of men and women in hierarchical medieval society.

3. In his analysis of the Middle Ages, Fromm argued that the Catholic church reflected both matriarchal and patriarchal elements in society. The first stressed unconditional love, mercy, and compassion; the second reward for good behaviour, repentance for going astray, and renewed submission. This was mirrored in the figure of Mary on the one hand and the role of the priest as father on the other.

Overall, "The medieval church stressed the dignity of man, the freedom of his will, and the fact that his efforts were of avail; it stressed the likeness between man and God and also man's right to be confident of God's love."[11]

This is the background to Fromm's view of the Reformation's protest against medieval church and society. Catholicism's emphasis on a patriarchal form of Christianity, with work as the only way to get love and approval, reflected the prevailing spirit among the aristocracy, emerging capitalists, artists, and philosophers, whose economic position gave them a sense of independence and power. Luther's gospel stressed the importance of individual trust in God's redemptive activity over against ecclesiastical authority and control of the means of salvation. Since its message was premised on man's innate predisposition towards evil and inner bondage to sin, salvation and spiritual growth can only be overcome by wholly trusting in an all-powerful God. This appealed to the hopes and expectations of the lower classes, especially the urban poor and rural peasants. In the long term, however, Luther's social conservatism limited the effectiveness of its partially revolutionary appeal.

Yet for the middle class, caught between the old feudal order and the rise of the new capitalists:

> *Luther's picture of man mirrored just this dilemma. Man is free from all ties binding him to spiritual authorities, but this very freedom leaves him alone and anxious ... The picture of man which he draws in religious terms describes the situation of the individual as it was brought about by the current social and economic evolution.*[12]

Unfortunately, says Fromm, this emphasis on submission to an absolute God proved to be even more tyrannical than the ecclesiastical one it replaced. In its essentials Calvin's theology was similar to Luther's and led to similar results. The only differences were minor. Calvin addressed the concerns of the middle class more uniformly and forcefully by touching chords of hostility and resentment against the wealthier groups. Meanwhile his doctrine of God predestining some to salvation emphasized more strongly man's uncertainty and insignificance, paradoxically placing greater stress upon post-conversion effort.

So then, the new religious doctrines of the two main reformers "not only gave expression to what the average member of the middle class felt but by rationalising and systematising this attitude, they also increased and strengthened it".[13]

In time, he adds, behind the Christian facade established by the Reformation, a new secret, "industrial" religion began to surface. For a long time this was not recognized as religion. Unlike genuine Christianity it reduces people to being servants of the economy and of the machines they have made. As such it is a new form of idolatry. He points out that many people who believe in God are idolatrous in their actual practices, whereas many atheists live in accord with humanistic religious ideals. For this reason, the time has come for religiously inclined people to stop arguing about God and concentrate on unmasking contemporary forms of idolatry.

Evaluating Fromm's approach

Aspects of Fromm's account have resonated with people on the spectrum between belief and unbelief in God. For example, many right along this spectrum have encountered authoritarian forms of religion at both the personal and institutional level. In doing so they have felt personally – even religiously – constrained, manipulated, exploited or victimized, and sometimes reacted against this by calling into question the kind of God called upon to validate this. In some cases, what such people went through in religious organizations was far worse than anything they had experienced in non-religious ones and that, in their worst moments, led to their temporarily or permanently doubting the reality of God.

In general, Fromm's approach is less immediately confronting than those of the earlier main representatives of the view that we created God we have examined. He is less aggressive towards religion and appears to give it more room to play. It is perhaps partly for this reason that he has had few disciples building on his general position. One figure who sympathizes with his general approach is the Australian philosopher Tamas Pataki, who in particular has reprised Fromm's views on how Christ attained divine status.[14] Other thinkers who have developed views on religion from a humanist perspective tend to show less interest in the question of how and why the idea of God arose. While Fromm's view of religion is more nuanced and comprehensive than the approaches we have looked at so far, like them it also raises some questions that require closer attention.

An initial, more general, one has to do with his difficulty in distinguishing between religious and ethical activity. Fromm himself admits that it is exceedingly difficult, and when he tries to do this problems appear. For him it is our "consciousness" of being alive and the question this raises that marks the difference, but could this not also be said of genuine ethical reflection? For him it is the "ultimacy" of ethical concern that betrays a religious dimension, but is this anything more than being genuinely rather than superficially ethical? For him it is "harmony" with oneself, others and the universe that distinguishes the two – but does doing this go beyond merely ethical questions about how we relate properly to each of these?

1. His view of God

Unlike his predecessors, Fromm recognizes the existence of positive and negative types of religion. His distinction between authoritarian and humanistic allows that some types of belief are not based on fantasy, escapism or neurosis. While authoritarian personalities regularly appear in religious contexts and popular religions often encourage over-dependent attitudes, the examples he gives of the two kinds of religion raise both historical and logical problems. For example, Isaiah could scarcely be said to conceive of God as "the symbol of man's powers" since he frequently remarks on the qualitative difference between God and humanity. Indeed of all the major Jewish prophets he is the one who constantly distinguishes between divine and human ways of thinking and acting.

Also questionable is Fromm's claim that the term "authoritarian" is the most appropriate overall description of Christianity. Its basic documents portray God extensively in loving, self-giving and ultimately sacrificial terms. He is represented in fatherly not tyrannical, paternal not paternalistic, devoted not arbitrary terms. Meanwhile those who relate to him are talked about as maturing adults with complex responsibilities, not as ever-dependent infants unable to fend for themselves. In this connection, one can also ask whether reliance on a higher power or divine being necessarily inhibits movement towards human potential. This is especially the case if it takes place through the Spirit residing within rather than outside people, and if it is love rather than force that empowers people to become who they were divinely designed to be.

Yet, inadequate as Fromm's distinction may be, it does open up the possibility of discussing religion in less monolithic terms. Likewise his recognition that there is a cognitive – as well as affective and volitional – dimension to belief in God is often lacking in psychological approaches. It also moves towards being more functional in character, evaluating religion by its effects rather than by its beliefs.

2. His understanding of psychological processes

Like Freud, Fromm generally views *projection* as a purely defensive psychological mechanism, though he regards it as closer to masochism than paranoia. But he goes beyond Freud in suggesting that projection, and corresponding self-alienation, occurs only in authoritarian forms of religion. Unfortunately, he does not go on to discuss sufficiently other more positive psychological mechanisms, or whether projection may occasionally be a valid process.

On the other hand, Fromm occasionally recognizes the limits of psychological enquiry more than his mentor does:

> *In studying the psychological significance of a religious ... or political doctrine we must first bear in mind that the psychological analysis does not imply a judgment concerning the truth of the doctrine one analyses. This latter question can be decided only in terms of the logical structure of the problem itself.*

Disappointingly he then qualifies this by adding that, as well as throwing light on people's psychic constitution and social circumstances, it "may itself uncover the real meaning of a doctrine and therefore influence one's value judgment".[15]

Interesting here is the primacy he gives to value over truth, and the genetic fallacy hovers uncertainly in the background. As we have seen, psychological investigation cannot locate the *causes* of a belief, only the psychological *context* in which it arose and the *character* it may have.

Fromm's introduction of a social dimension into the psychological study of religion is certainly an advance on Freud. This allows him to view commitment to God in a wider interpersonal and institutional framework rather than one dominated by the father and sexuality. However, he does not allow that this could reflect a divine structure to which people must relate if they are to discover their full divine potential. Instead, like Freud, he tends to dismiss belief in God, even within the framework of a humanistic form of religion, as "infantile" in character and therefore to be overcome. But, as we have seen, this is not necessarily the case. While some past and present religious experience exhibits immature tendencies, not all dependent relationships need be of this kind. We see this in the Old Testament where, taking up God's invitation, people are portrayed as negotiating (Abraham), reasoning (Isaiah) and radically questioning (Job) God. In the New Testament too, as in Paul's first letter to the Corinthians, believers are encouraged to leave behind childish things and become adult in their thinking (14:20).[16]

3. His understanding of social factors

Fromm's views are also an advance on Marx, for he does not regard religion as simply a reflection of social and economic conditions. Apart from what it is psychologically, a wider set of sociological factors affect the form religion takes in any particular period.[17] But in two respects Fromm does not go far enough. In the first place, he does not recognize the innovative character of belief in God down through the centuries. Fromm could have drawn here on the correction of Marx referred to earlier by the well-known social philosophers Max Weber (1864–1920) and R. H. Tawney (1880–1962), both of whom acknowledged the direct role of ideas in historical change and development.

In his account of the way views of God have developed over time, Fromm also tends to allow social and economic factors too dominant a place. His interpretation of developing views of Jesus' divinity in *The Dogma of Christ* during the first few centuries, and of changes in the understanding of God in the late medieval and early modern period, both come to mind here. Despite his recognizing the presence of a cognitive element in religion, he makes no room for this in his discussion. The views of the key religious thinkers and groups cannot be fitted into a purely socio-economic framework. Some of the detailed studies of changing views of God in these two periods acknowledge the impact of wider cultural influences but do not reduce such discussions to them.[18]

Fromm's ambiguous legacy

As we have seen, Fromm's approach opens up the possibility of a more nuanced and discriminating approach to religion in general and to the idea of God in particular. He seeks to integrate psychological as well as sociological factors in discussing the origin and development of religious beliefs. He recognizes that belief in God can have cognitive as well as emotional content. However, this integration does not include the role of other aspects of life, and this recognition does not go beyond discussing the psychological presuppositions of certain beliefs.

His limited view of projection is also a problem here. As Peter Berger has argued, depending on the frame of reference something can be both a human projection and a reflection of reality at the same time. He provides a good example of what he means from mathematics:

> *The mathematics that man projects out of his own consciousness somehow corresponds to a mathematical reality that is external to him, and indeed which his consciousness appears to reflect. How is this possible? It is possible, of course, because man himself is part of the same overall reality, so that there is a fundamental affinity between the structures of his consciousness and the structures of the empirical world. Projection and reflection are movements within the same encompassing reality. The same may be true of the projections of man's religious imagination.*[19]

A question could still be asked here. On Berger's premises, could not "projection" itself be just as much an instrument of divine activity through human beings?

As mentioned earlier, Fromm's distinction between authoritarian and humanistic religion is helpful and certainly an improvement on earlier one-dimensional views of it. But it is not fully adequate. His view of humankind and of human empowerment is still too simplistic. At fault here is not just the way he interprets the views of some religious thinkers and traditions but his basic humanist perspective. He lacks a more complex set of criteria that does not polarize dependence on others and individual autonomy, divine-centred obedience and self-fulfilment, but instead develops a more complex account of their relationship.

Fromm, in line with anthropological thinking more generally, also rightly rejects Freud's mythological theory of religious origins and of an inherited racial unconscious. But in doing this he tends to make religion a less primary and profound dimension of life. This prevents his account from getting inside, and plumbing the depths of, the religious experience of not only formative figures, but also ordinary believers. His view of humankind pays less attention to the darker aspects of human behaviour and focuses too much on the extent to which it is ego-directed. This betrays a shallower approach to religion stemming from Fromm's more optimistic humanist convictions.

Yet, whatever the deficiencies of Fromm's view, especially in its dismissal of God as a man-made creation, it still raises valid questions as to how much religion is made over by its adherents. To that we can now give our full attention.

PART FOUR

A TIME FOR SELF-EXAMINATION

8

FACING UP TO THE PERSONAL CHALLENGE

All too often these major critics of religion are viewed merely as opponents of belief in God. Even if their view that God is altogether an imaginary human creation does not stand up, to some degree or other everyone's religious beliefs contain man-made elements. They may not have been the first to propose this but they did so in a more detailed and substantial way. In this respect they build on the insights of earlier Christian and rationalist critics of religion. It is interesting here to note that all four of these figures come from a culturally religious background: Feuerbach grew up in a Protestant family, Marx in one that had converted from Judaism to a nominal Protestantism, Freud and Fromm in non-observing secular Jewish contexts. Though the influence of their backgrounds varied, and in significant ways each thinker reacted against his background, their Jewish and/or Christian upbringing undoubtedly played a part in shaping their outlooks.

One indicator of this is their engagement with some of the most important Jewish and Christian figures and movements. Feuerbach interacts in a general way with systematic theology and in a more detailed way with Luther's writings. Fromm gives extensive attention to the Old Testament and to the development of Jewish and Christian ideas. In particular he singles out false representations of God as a category for evaluating contemporary forms of religious and non-religious belief. For their part, Marx and Freud could be described as religiously influenced secular prophets who, in differing degrees, investigated the role of religious belief and practice in past and present societies.

The ongoing relevance of this critique of God

Where these major critics specifically focus on the religious beliefs and attitudes of the mass of people, they deserve close attention and we should listen to them carefully. For from many angles they expose the questionable character of civic, nominal, or superficial belief in God. But since even committed, self-aware, and knowledgeable believers tend to infuse their personal preferences into their ideas of God, they have something to say to these as well. What follows in this chapter explores how these secular critics can help us to identify and discard any elements of what may be described as "instrumental religion, the piety that reduces God to a means or instrument for achieving our own human purposes with professedly divine power and sanction".[1] In this area, if we understand these critics rightly, we may view them as "the great secular theologians of original sin".[2]

Whether people are believers or not, they have an endemic inclination to impose something of what suits their own concerns on their positive or negative view of God. Human beings have a constant temptation to project their own wishes and fears onto whatever idea of God they derive from other sources. The reason for this is that by so doing they create an image of the divine over which they can retain control.

> *Idols are indispensable for mankind. We need to see things represented and make the powers enter our domain of idolatry. It is a sort of kidnapping … things that can be seen and grasped are certain and at our disposition … If … a person makes his own image and can certify that it is the deity, he is no longer afraid.*[3]

This helps unbelievers to avoid coming to terms with the God who is really there, and it helps believers dilute what he is really like. In both cases, it enables them to sidestep the genuine claims God might make upon them. In addition, it enables them to harness unbelief or belief for their own, rather than what are actually or potentially divine, purposes.

Some religious thinkers have directly addressed this issue. One already noted is Karl Barth, with his judgment on nineteenth-century theology. Its focus on human consciousness rather than divine revelation has continued up until our own time, as the writings of the widely read John Shelby Spong demonstrate. But Barth also had in mind believers who possessed a more traditional understanding of God. As well as allowing other things into their lives to which they give idolatrous status, they can also fall prey to substituting their own ideas of God for what God himself reveals. They can become so preoccupied with "their religious needs" that they develop "comfortable illusions" about God and their relationship with him.[4] Even when they seek to be dependent on divine revelation and treat it as purely objective,[5] they can unconsciously edit the Bible, deleting things about God they would prefer not to find, or turning what the Bible says about God into something more congenial to their thinking.

According to Barth, because of the human tendency to make God in our own image, believers should point the finger at themselves before they do so at unbelievers, for "[it] is firstly a problem for the Church, not for others".[6] They should enquire into "beliefs and behaviours which are a betrayal of the true allegiance God invites, in order that God may be known more truly".[7]

The Catholic theologian Nicholas Lash agrees: "Christian doctrine ... functions, or should function, as a set of protocols against idolatry. The critical ... task is ... the critique of idolatry – the stripping away of the veils of self-assurance by which we seek to protect our faces from exposure to the mystery of God."[8] For Lash, idolatry involves what consists in falsely according an aspect of creaturely reality absolute significance. This results from the misdirected devotion of the core values, commitments and priorities that shape our whole lives, not just what we regard as the religious part of them. It all comes down to what we have set our hearts on. This can be an object, experience or person, and this is sometimes cloaked in religious terms. Because people tend to put their faith in more than one direction, most are in practice "polytheists",[9] even when they claim to focus their lives on God.[10] But God "is not, and never can be, one of a number of possible objects of consideration and use".[11]

This does not mean an either/or choice between giving ourselves to him and giving ourselves to others. Since he is the one on whom everything depends and who gives meaning to everything, making God central in one's life embraces loving and serving others, as well as engaging the whole of life and nature, in and through him. For: "Everything we do and suffer, enact and tolerate and undergo, all the good and evil that we do, contribute either to our proximity or distance from God."[12]

This is where those who believe in God can learn from the four main figures just discussed, for they clearly signpost some of the key ways God may be domesticated.

- Regarding Feuerbach, they should examine whether their image of God is overly influenced by their religious dreams and fantasies, or by their wishes and longings about their individual potential or expectations of community. They should also examine whether they regard God's providence too much in terms of his being a kind of super guardian angel, or view Christ too much as the sum of human excellence as they understand this rather than as the one who defines what it actually involves.

- Regarding Marx, they should reflect on how much their idea of God is simply a compensation for things they lack in this life or unjustly or involuntarily suffer. Or, if they are members of a more privileged group in society, how much their idea of God is shaped by a sense of preferential treatment, a dominant role, and automatic blessing of their material endeavours.

- Regarding Freud, they should query how much their picture of God is adversely affected by their relationship with their parents. How much does God exist for them mainly to offer them protection and guarantee them a comfortable future, without having to worry about much else? And how much does their faith give them a reason to serve God in appearance when in fact they are satisfying their own interests, needs and guilt feelings?[13]

- Regarding Fromm, to what extent is their view of God authoritarian rather than merely authoritative in character? In what measure do they think of God as acting manipulatively or coercively rather than sensitively or even firmly towards them? How far do they understand God as wanting to force them to do his will instead of wooing and challenging them to develop what they believe to be the creative gifts he has given them and character traits he is cultivating within them?

Concrete examples of the problem

In what follows I will look first at the most widely held images of God and then at the most common substitutes for God that are current today.

1. Popular images of God

In his widely read book, *Your God is Too Small*, J. B. Phillips lists some of the most common images of God that regulate people's attitudes across the whole spectrum of belief and unbelief. These include God being seen as:

- Resident Policeman

- Parental Hangover

- Grand Old Man

- Absolute Perfectionist

- Heavenly Bosom

- Perennial Disappointer

Other images that he identifies include:

- Busy God

- Elite God

- Contractual God

- God-in-a-Box[14]

Many of these have an element of truth within them. But this has been distorted by inadequate human perceptions of these images, stretching them beyond their proper boundaries, or viewing them through a limiting cultural lens.

It would not be difficult to add other images of God to these, some of which have had a long history and some of which have appeared more recently. For example, God as:

- Authoritarian Teacher

- Santa Claus

- Divine Mr Fix-It

- Ecclesiastical CEO

- Universal Dad

- Charismatic Magician

- Intimate Counsellor

- Militaristic Warrior

- Backstage Manager

- Exclusive Sectarian

- Hyper-Activist

- Vindictive Torturer

- Impotent Bystander

- Religious Idealogue

- Dogmatic Theologian

- Big Brother

- Patriotic Chaplain

- Moral Accountant

- Male Chauvinist

- White Supremacist

- Spoilsport

- Guardian Angel

- Eternal Life Insurer

In some of these images it is hard to find any link to traditional views of God. In others it is there but deeply hidden, obscured, or distorted. Often people's behaviour is governed by more than one image. When this happens, one image may dominate more than another, a few may assume greater or lesser importance according to mood and circumstances, and contrary images may sometimes lie inconsistently alongside one another. Specific subcultures can sometimes entertain profiles of God that distinguish them from others.

According to the sociologist Christian Smith, the profile of God among the younger generation of seekers and believers reflects cultural more than religious values. This means that they believe:

- God wants people to be good, nice, and fair to each other;

- God's basic desire for people is to be happy and to feel good about themselves;

- God does not need to be particularly involved in their life, except when needed to resolve a problem.[15]

The pervasiveness of certain cultural values today makes it all too easy to think of God in overly individualistic or intimate terms, and to portray God functioning by means of characteristic metaphors of our age drawn from the world of technology or the environment.

2. Popular substitutes for God

It is not only by means of these popular images and values that the idea of God can undergo a smaller or larger makeover. There are also the alternative gods people create and set up for themselves. Almost anything can play this role, including ourselves. In examining the writings of the four main representatives of the critique of religion as man-made, there is already a tendency to deify humanity, as well as the granting of a kind of idolatrous status to the methods of anthropology, historical materialism, scientistic psychology or some combination of these. Other examples identified by various writers over the last century include:

- tradition, institution, possession, ideal (Nicholas Lash);

- nature, civilization, materialism, secularism, church, democracy (Karl Barth);

- sacred buildings, money, technology (Jacques Ellul);

- revolution, nationalism, prosperity, security (Bob Goudzward);

- humanity, history, power (Herman Schlossberg);

- relevance, change, liberation (Kenneth Hamilton);

- love, money, success, power (Tim Keller);

- romance, beauty, success, reputation, family, education, celebrity, performance (Julian Hardyman).

What all these have in common is that they provide a more tangible and concrete focus for our lives. Even where they seem more abstract – like romance, success, idealism, change, and humanity – they have concrete embodiments on which we fix our attention. The distinction between deep and surface idols is helpful here and most often people's god substitutes are a mixture of the two. Although these are substitutes for God rather than attributes of God, it is worthwhile including them here. For some of these too can be attached to God as a necessary part of what he is about.

Overcoming man-made views of God

How can even religiously committed people avoid imagining God in their own image?

1. The first thing is to carefully choose the major weapon for confronting and neutralizing it. But in order to do this, as Barth said of Feuerbach: "No one can strike him with it unless he himself has been hit with it. This argument is no mere weapon that one exploits in apologetics, it should be a ground on which one can stand, and with fear and trembling allow to speak for itself."[16]

In other words, a person has to allow the full force of the view that God is a man-made creation to fall upon them. Having done that, the only way they can avoid falling into this error is to ensure that "the whole line of relation to God is one that is in principle incontrovertible".[17]

There are two main dangers here. The first is to distinguish God and humankind so completely that God is always "the transcendent other" who differs from human beings in every respect. This makes it hard to find any criteria for judging the validity of one portrait of God over another. If, for example, God's justice is completely different from ours, is it not possible to depict him in ways that are quite monstrous?

The second is to reject clues to the nature of God that are revealed through creation and in Man. After all, the creation is the result of his handiwork and all people are made in his image. However affected these may be by what the Bible describes as the Fall, and however much people need God's additional revelation in the Bible to enlighten them, echoes of God are present both in human beings and in the created order.

2. Second, believers must draw on the life and teaching of Christ as central to their understanding of God. In the face of their tendency to produce an idolatrous representation of God, they have instead his own true image, Jesus Christ. He is

the one who not only demonstrates true deity but, through the power of his death and resurrection, frees them from the false god substitutes. Their next task is to ensure that this overcoming of the idols becomes transparent in their thinking and living. Indeed they must become iconoclasts, destroyers of the contemporary forms that man-made versions of, or substitutes for, God take. Otherwise they will not be able to help others see through them and become more open to discovering the real thing. Indeed, of all people: "We live in a world that, to the same extent that it more and more rejects the Christian faith, also fabricates for itself more and more idols and ... Christians have an enormous service to render here."[18]

Once again, however, there are two dangers. First, they must be careful not to contemporize Jesus so much that his true character is obscured. Since every age looks at Jesus through its own cultural lens, they cannot altogether avoid doing this. But if they are aware of the temptation, and cross-examine their understanding with the help of past and present viewpoints, they can minimize the difficulty.

Second, they must reject the tendency in some circles today to place Jesus so much in the centre that the Father is pushed into the background. This is related to Freud's view of a religion of the Father being replaced by that of the Son. This is a particular temptation for younger shakers and movers on the religious scene and for those who have not fully grown up in their understanding.

It is not uncommon to read mission statements, promotions of events, even brief statements of faith, which do not mention, or scarcely mention, the overall Father at all.

3. They should make use of available psychological, sociological and cultural analyses to help them understand themselves, their world, and the interplay between these and their beliefs and practice. But it is important to avoid incautious human analogies for God or overly depending on purely negative ways of describing him. It is also important to encourage people's desire for God rather than possession of him, and to help them experience the all-transforming power of God's Spirit in impacting the world rather than withdrawing from it or only trying to draw people in a heavenly direction out of it.

4. Ultimately this must be embodied in more than words, as only through the personal and corporate lives of believers "can the reality of God be persuasively displayed".[19] It has to be lived and demonstrated.

One of the most compelling examples of this comes again from the life of C. S. Lewis, whom I have already quoted in this book. This happened in response to the suffering he experienced after his wife Joy died of cancer. In a series of notebooks that were eventually issued as *A Grief Observed* he poured out a volatile range of emotions. In the midst of this, he portrayed God as first the Cruel Gaoler who double-bolts the door leading to himself, then as the Great Vivisector who cuts a person in half by taking away the one they love, and then as the Cosmic Sadist who delights in the pain he causes his creatures.

Over a period of time, however, he came to see that part of what he was struggling with was his idea of God rather than God himself. Up till then he had thought this was shaped by what he had learned in one way or another from God. But now he realized that:

> *My idea of God is not a divine idea. It has to be*
> *shattered time after time. He shatters it Himself.*
> *He is the great iconoclast. Could we not say that*
> *this shattering is one of the marks of His presence?*
> *The Incarnation is the supreme example; it leaves*
> *all previous ideas of the Messiah in ruins. And most*
> *are "offended" by the iconoclasm, and blessed are*
> *those that are not. But the same thing happens in*
> *our private prayers.*

He goes on to point out that there is nothing exceptional in this purely because God is different from us. For, in fact, all reality is iconoclastic. The one you love in this life triumphs over your mere idea of her. This is also the case of everything you want of her, for you want her with all her differences, resistances, faults, surprisingness. This means that with respect to continuing to love both her and God:

> *I must stretch out the arms and hands of love*
> *through all the changeful fantasies of my thoughts,*
> *passions and imaginings ... [So] ... Not my idea*
> *of God, but God ... And all this time I may, once*
> *more, be building with cards. And if I am He will*
> *once more knock the building flat. He will knock it*
> *down as long as it proves necessary.*[20]

With this, Lewis provides an example for everyone interested in the God issue, both those wondering if he exists and those convinced that he does. For the first group, finding out whether God is real or not involves more than just thinking about it and weighing up the evidence. It involves actively engaging with the possibility that he is there by relating to God as if he might actually be a conversation partner.

This means asking God questions, declaring to God one's objections, crying out to God in suffering, and challenging God to respond in some concrete way.

For the second group, as Lewis demonstrates, it involves more than just assuming one's image of him is always well founded. It also involves interrogating God when there are uncertainties, laying before God one's doubts, crying out to God when injustice seems to be taking place, and challenging God to respond in a quite personal way.

Only in this way can both seeker and believer find out whether God is really there and whether he is really as they imagine. The confidence to do this lies in the conclusion that emerges from the investigation in this book: that the one best placed to determine whether any idea of God is man-made or not is actually the God-who-became-man himself.

Notes

Chapter 1

1. Steve Toltz, *A Fraction of the Whole*, Camberwell: Penguin, 2008, p. 125.
2. Stephen Hawking, *A Brief History of Time*, London: Bantam, 1988.
3. For example, David E. Comings, *Did Man Create God? Is Your Spiritual Brain at Peace with Your Thinking Brain?*, Duarte CA: Hope Press, 2008.
4. Richard Dawkins, *The God Delusion*, London: Bantam, 2006, p. 109.
5. Sam Harris, *Letter to a Christian Nation*, London: Bantam, 2007, pp. 55, 73.
6. Daniel Dennett, *Darwin's Dangerous Idea*, London: Penguin, 1996, p. 18, and further *The End of Faith: Religion, Terror and the Future of Reason*, New York: Norton, 2004.
7. André Comte Sponville, *The Book of Atheist Spirituality*, London: Bantam, 2008.
8. Christopher Hitchens, *God is Not Great: How Religion Poisons Everything*, London and Sydney: Allen & Unwin, 2007, p. 9.
9. Michael Onfray, *The Atheist Manifesto: The Case Against Christianity, Judaism and Islam*, Melbourne: Melbourne University Press, 2007.
10. Bertrand Russell, *God and Religion*, Tonbridge: Prometheus, 1986, p. 60.

11. Bertrand Russell, "A Free Man's Worship" in *Mysticism and Logic and Other Essays*, London: Allen & Unwin, 1951, pp. 48–50.

12. Russell's place in the historical development of anti-religious views is explored in David Berman, *A History of Atheism in Britain: From Hobbes to Russell*, London: Routledge, 1991.

13. Stewart Elliott Guthrie, *Faces in the Clouds: A New Theory of Religion*, Oxford: Oxford University Press, 1993.

14. Karen Armstrong, *A History of God From Abraham to the Present: The 4000-Year Quest for God*, London: Mandarin, 1999, p. 60.

15. C. S. Lewis, *Surprised by Joy*, London: Collins, 1935, pp. 3, 22–23.

16. Reported in "God is a Lot Like You", *The Sydney Morning Herald*, 2 December 2009.

Chapter 2

1. See Habakkuk 2:18–19; Hosea 7:14. For earlier references to the gods, see on the one hand Exodus 20:3 and on the other 1 Chronicles 16:26; Judges 6:31. An entry view is argued by Mark S. Smith, *The Early History of God: Yahweh and Other Deities in Ancient Israel*, 2nd edn, Grand Rapids: Eerdmans, 2002.

2. Deuteronomy 4:28; 32:21.

3. Jeremiah 10:4, 9.

4. Jeremiah 10:5, 14–15; 16:20.

5. Jeremiah 50:6, 17; 18:15.

6. Jeremiah 50:38.

7. Ezekiel 16:17, 20, 24.

8. Ezekiel 22:26, 31; 36:20; 44:23.

9. Ezekiel 13; 28:28; 44:10.

10. Isaiah 40:18–20; 44:10–20; 46:1–2.

11. Isaiah 41:29; 44:20.
12. Isaiah 44:18.
13. *Letter of Jeremiah*, v. 29.
14. Philo, *The Decalogue* XIV.66 – XVI.81.
15. Philo, *De Spec. Leg.* 1.V.29.
16. On this subject generally see A. B. Drachmann, *Atheism in Pagan Antiquity*, London: Glydenhal, 1922 and J. Thrower, *The Alternative Tradition: A Study of Unbelief in the Ancient World*, The Hague: Mouton, 1980.
17. W. Jaeger, *The Theology of the Early Greek Philosophers*, Oxford: Oxford University Press, 1957, p. 174.
18. FV.II.B.14–16
19. Plato, *Laws*, 889.
20. FV.55.B.166.
21. Philodemus, *De piet*. c.9, 51.
22. *Sextus Empiricus*, Ad. Math. 9.18; 51–52.
23. *Sextus Empiricus*, Math. 9.54.
24. Maimonides, *Code of Jewish Laws*, Laws of Idolatry I.
25. Moshe Halbertal and Avishai Magalit, *Idolatry*, Cambridge: Harvard Univerity Press, 1992, 109.
26. Maimonides, *Guide for the Perplexed*, I.36.

Chapter 3

1. Acts 17:16–34.
2. Romans 1:16–25; 1 Corinthians 8:4; 10:20.
3. Justin Martyr, *First Apology* VI, XXV; *Hortatory Address to the Greeks*, XXXIV, XXXVIII
4. Tatian, *Address to the Greeks* XVI–XVIII; Athenagoras, *Hortatory Address to the Greeks*, XXXIV, XXXVIII.
5. Clement, *Miscellanies*, II.25.4 – 26.8.
6. Lactantius, *The Divine Institutes*, I.15–22.
7. Ibid., II.1.
8. Ibid., II.3, pp. 15–19.

9. Athanasius, *Against the Heathens*, 3.1–2.

10. Athanasius, *On the Incarnation*, 8.1–3.

11. Ibid., 19.1.

12. VII.34.

13. F. van der Meer, *Augustine the Bishop: The Life and Work of a Father of the Church*, Kansas City, New York: Harper & Row, 1961, p. 32.

14. Martin Luther, *Lectures on Romans: Luther's Works*, Vol. 25, St Louis: Concordia, 1972, p. 159.

15. Martin Luther, *Lectures on Isaiah ch.40–66*, St Louis: Concordia, 1972, 140; *Lectures on Romans*, pp. 158–160.

16. John Calvin, *Institutes of the Christian Religion*, Philadelphia: Westminster, 1960, I.11.80. On this generally, as well as the views of his predecessor, see Carlos M. N. Eire, *War Against the Idols: The Reformation of Worship from Erasmus to Calvin*, Cambridge: Cambridge University Press, 1986.

17. Ibid., I, 11.8.

18. William Perkins, "A warning against the idolatrie of the last times", in I. Breward (ed.), *The Works of William Perkins*, Appleby: Sutton-Coutrney, 1970, p. 275.

19. See A. B. Grossart (ed.) *The Complete Works of Richard Sibbes*, Edinburgh: James Nichol, 1862, II, p. 180 and see generally pp. 178–82, 382–85.

20. Pierre Bayle, "Reponse aux questions d'un provincial", *Oeuvres Diverses*, III, 1715, pp. 560–61.

21. David Hume, "The Natural History of Religion", in Richard Wollheim (ed.), *Hume on Religion*, London & Glasgow: Fontana, 1963, pp. 62–63.

22. Baron d'Holbach, *The System of Nature*, tr. H. D. Robinson, vol. 1, Boston: J. P. Mendum, 1868, p. 264.

23. Michael J. Buckley, *At the Origins of Modern Atheism*, Yale: Yale University Press, 2004.

24. D. G. McLeod, *Then Man Created God: The Truth About Believing a Lie*, Bloomington, Indiana: AuthorHouse, 2009.

Chapter 4

1. Ludwig Feuerbach, *Lectures on the Essence of Religion*, 1848–49, New York: Harper & Row, 1967, Lecture 20.
2. Ibid., xxxix.
3. Ludwig Feuerbach, *Collected Works*, Leipzig: O. Wigand, 1859, IX, p. 21.
4. Ludwig Feuerbach, *The Essence of Christianity*, San Francisco: Harper, 1953, p. 13.
5. Ibid., pp. 21–22, 27, 33.
6. Ibid., p. 48.
7. Ibid., p. 140. See further Eugene Kamenka, *The Philosophy of Ludiwg Feuerbach*, London: Routledge & Kegan Paul, 1970. On Feuerbach generally see further W. Wartofsky, *Feuerbach*, Cambridge: Cambridge University Press, 1982.
8. Karl Barth, *Protestant Theology in the Nineteenth Century: Its Background and History*, London: SCM, 1972, p. 234.
9. Fritz Buri, *The Theology of Existence*, Dublin: Attic Press, 1965.
10. Don Cupitt, *Taking Leave of God*, London: SCM, 1981, and in several other works. Paul van Buren, *The Secular Meaning of the Gospel*, New York: Macmillan, 1965.
11. C. S. Lewis, "'Bulverism', or the Foundation of 20th Century Thought", in Walter Hooper (ed.), *God in the Dock: Essays on Theology and Ethics*, Grand Rapids: Eerdmans, 1970, p. 212. On the following point see also C. S. Lewis, *The Problem of Pain*, London: Fontana, 1957, p. 9.

12. C. S. Lewis, *Mere Christianity*, Bk 1, ch. 5.
13. See Van A. Harvey, *Feuerbach and the Interpretation of Religion*, Cambridge: Cambridge University Press, 1995, and the critique by Charles D. Hardwick, "Harvey's Feuerbach and the Possibility of Liberal Theology", *Journal of the American Academy of Religion*, 66/4, 1996, pp. 863–885.
14. K. Barth, "An Introductory Essay" in *Ludwig Feuerbach, The Essence of Christianity*, San Francisco: Harper, 1957.
15. Ibid., xxiv.
16. Daniel F. Hardy and David W. Ford, *Praising and Knowing God*, Philadelphia: Westminster, pp. 109–110.

Chapter 5

1. Saul D. Padover (ed.), *Karl Marx on Religion*, New York: McGraw-Hill, 1974, pp. 235–36.
2. Ibid., p. 33.
3. Ibid., p. 35.
4. Ibid., pp. 4–5.
5. See generally D. M. McKown, *The Classic Marxist Critiques of Religion: Marx, Engels, Lenin, Kautsky*, The Hague: Martinus Nijhof, 1975.
6. Karl Lowith, "Man's Self-Alienation in the Early Writings of Marx", *Social Research*, XXI, Summer, 1954, p. 204.
7. *Karl Marx On Religion*, p. 35.
8. Ibid., p. 37.
9. Ibid., p. 36.
10. Ibid.
11. Ibid., p. 42.
12. Ibid., p. 36.
13. Ibid.
14. Ibid., p. 65.

15. Karl Marx and Friedrich Engels, *On Religion*, Moscow: Foreign Languages Publishing House, 1957, p. 136.

16. Gerd Ladner, *The Idea of Reform: Its Impact on Christian Thought and Action in the Age of the Fathers*, New York: Harvard University Press, 1967.

17. David Bentley Hart, *Atheist Delusions: The Christian Revolution and its Fashionable Enemies*, New Haven: Yale University Press, 2009, xi. cf. also pp. 30, 63, 98, 124, 171–74, 213–14.

18. On these developments see further John White Jr, *The Reformation of Rights: Law, Religion and Human Rights in Early Modern Calvinism*, Cambridge: Cambridge University Press, 2002, and James Hannam, *God's Philosophers: How the Medieval World Lay the Foundation for Modern Science*, London: Icon, 2009, respectively.

19. Jurgen Moltmann, "The Resurrection of Christ and the New Earth", in Keith Dyer and David Neville (eds), *Resurrection and Responsibility*, Eugene: Pickwick, 2009.

20. Robert Tucker, *Philosophy and Myth in Karl Marx*, Cambridge: Cambridge University Press, 1961, p. 22.

21. Alasdair MacIntyre, *Marxism and Christianity*, London: Penguin, 1968, p. 83.

Chapter 6

1. *The Psychopathology of Everyday Life*, New York: Norton, 1965, pp. 258–59.

2. "Leonardo da Vinci and a Memory of his Childhood", *Collected Works*, XI, 1910, p. 123

3. *The Psychopathology of Everyday Life*, p. 9.

4. *Moses and Monotheism*, New York: Vintage, 1955, p. 167.

5. Ibid., p. 174.

6. *The Future of an Illusion*, New York: Norton, 1961, p. 25.

7. Ibid., p. 30.

8. Ibid., p. 31.

9. Ibid., pp. 31, 33.

10. *Civilisation and its Discontents*, New York: Norton, 1961, p. 18.

11. Sigmund Freud, "An Autobiographical Study", *Complete Works*, Vol. 20, 1925–26, p. 70.

12. Isaiah 1:18; 1 Thessalonians 5:21.

13. William W. Meissner, *Psychoanalysis and Religious Experience*, Yale: Yale University Press, 1986. In relation to religious origins where fresh thinking has taken place – as in Richard Clark, *The Multiple Natural Origins of Religion*, Oxford: Peter Lang, 2006 – it has tended to recognize the more complex nature of the matter.

14. Gordon Allport, *The Individual and His Religion: A Psychological Interpretation*, New York: Macmillan, 1951, p. 60.

15. *Civilisation and its Discontents*, p. 11.

16. Ana-Maria Rizzuto, *The Birth of the Living God: A Psychoanalytic Study*, Chicago: University of Chicago Press, 1979, especially chapters 2 and 10.

17. Ana-Maria Rizzuto, *Why Did Freud Reject God? A Psychodynamic Interpretation*, Yale: Yale Univeristy Press, 1998. A more straightforward biographical account of Freud may be found in Peter Gay, *A Godless Jew: Freud, Atheism and the Making of Psychoanalysis*, Yale: Yale University Press, 1987.

18. On the following see the earlier summary of Paul Kline, *Fact and Fantasy in Freudian Theory*, London: Methuen, 1972, pp. 348, 34ff; and the more recent one provided by Michael Argyle, *Theories of Religious Belief, Experience and Behaviour*, London: Routledge, 1997, pp. 183–87.

19. See also A. Vergote & A. Tamayo, *The Parental Figures as the Representation of God: A Psychological and Cross-Cultural Study*, The Hague: Mouton, 1981.

20. Fokke Sierksma, *The Religious Projection*, 1956, and *The Gods as We Shape Them*, 1960.

21. Leopold Bwellak and Lawrence Abt, *Projective Psychology: Clinical Approaches to the Total Personality*, New York: Alfred Knopf, 1950.

22. Allport, *The Individual and His Religion*, p. 122.

23. Cf. H. Meng and E. L. Freud (eds), *Psychoanalysis and Faith: The Letters of Sigmund Freud and Oscar Pfister*, London: Hogarth, 1963, p. 117.

24. Phillip Rieff, *The Mind of a Moralist*, Chicago: University of Chicago Press, 1959, p. 257.

25. Antoine Vergote, "What the psychology of religion is and what it is not", *International Journal of Psychology of Religion*, vol. 3, 1993, pp. 73–86.

26. See further A. N. Nicholi Jr, *The Question of God: C. S. Lewis and Sigmund Freud Debate God, Love, Sex, and the Meaning of Life*, New York: Free Press, 2002, p. 51.

Chapter 7

1. Erich Fromm, *Psychoanalysis and Religion*, New York: Bantam, 1950, p. 22.

2. Ibid., p. 26.

3. Ibid., pp. 48–49. Cf. *Man for Himself*, London: Routledge & Kegan Paul, 1948, pp. 197–210.

4. *Psychoanalysis and Religion*, pp. 50–51.

5. *You Shall Be as Gods: A Radical Interpretation of the Old Testament and its Tradition*, New York: Fawcett, 1967, p. 23.

6. Ibid., p. 32.

7. Ibid., p. 39.

8. Ibid., p. 49.

9. Erich Fromm, "The Dogma of Christ and Other Essays" in *Psychology, Religion and Culture*, London: Routledge & Kegan Paul, 1963, p. 67.

10. Ibid., p. 48.

11. Erich Fromm, *Escape from Freedom*, New York: Avon, 1941, p. 92.

12. Ibid., pp. 99–100.

13. Ibid., p. 121.

14. Tamas Pataki, *Against Religion*, Melbourne: Melbourne University Press, 2007, especially pp. 54–70.

15. *Fear of Freedom*, pp. 53–54.

16. Compare 1 Corinthians 13:11

17. J. H. Schaar, *Escape from Authority: The Perspectives of Erich Fromm*, New York: Basic Books, 1961, p. 126.

18. See, for example, H. J. Carpenter, *Popular Christianity and the Early Theologies*, Philadelphia: Fortress, p. 196.

19. Peter Berger, *A Rumour of Angels: Modern Society and the Rediscovery of the Supernatural*, New York: Anchor, 1969, p. 58, and more generally *The Sacred Canopy: Elements of a Sociological Theory of Religion*, New York: Anchor, 1967.

Chapter 8

1. Merold Westphal, *Suspicion and Faith: The Religious Uses of Modern Atheism*, Grand Rapids: Eerdmans, 1993, p. 6.

2. Ibid., p. 288.

3. Jacques Ellul, *Humiliation of the Word*, Grand Rapids: Eerdmans, 1985, p. 89.

4. Karl Barth, *The Epistle to the Romans*, New York: Oxford University Press, 1933, p. 37.

5. Karl Barth, *Church Dogmatics*, Edinburgh: T & T Clark, I/1, 1936, 257, I/2, 1936, pp. 353; 846.

6. David Clough, "Karl Barth on Religious and Irreligious

Idolatry", in S. C. Barton (ed.), *Idolatry: False Worship in the Bible, Early Judaism and Christianity*, Edinburgh: T & T Clark, 2007, p. 227.

7. S. C. Barton (ed.), *Idolatry: False Worship in the Bible, Early Judaism and Christianity,* Edinburgh: T & T Clark, 2007, p. 1.

8. Nicholas Lash, *The Beginning and End of "Religion"*, Cambridge: Cambridge University Press, 1996, p. 194.

9. Ibid.

10. Ibid., pp. 20–21.

11. Nicholas Lash, *Easter in Ordinary: Reflections on Human Experience and the Knowledge of God*, London: SCM, 1988, p. 196.

12. Nicholas Lash, *Believing Three Ways in One God: A Reading of the Apostles' Creed*, London: SCM, 1992, p. 100.

13. On what we can learn from Freud about false religion see further the analysis by the theologian Paul Tillich in John M. Perry, *Tillich's Response to Freud: A Christian Answer to the Freudian Critique of Religion*, Rowan and Littlefield, 1988.

14. J. B. Phillips, *Your God is Too Small*, London: Epworth, 1962. See more recently J. Haberer, *God Views: The Convictions that Drive and Divide Us*, Louisville, KY: Geneva Press, 2001, and Miroslav Volf, *Free of Charge: Giving and Receiving in a Culture Stripped of Grace*, Grand Rapids: Zondervan, 2005, pp. 21–28.

15. Christian Smith, *Soul Searching: The Religious and Spiritual Lives of American Teenagers*, New York: Oxford University Press, 2005.

16. K. Barth, "An Introductory Essay" in Ludwig Feuerbach, *The Essence of Christianity*, San Francisco: Harper, 1957.

17. Ibid., p. xxiii.

18. Jacques Ellul, "Christian Faith and Social Reality", in Marva Dawn (ed.), in *Sources and Trajectories*, Grand Rapids: Eerdmans, 1997, p. 176. See further Miroslav Volf, Free of Charge, p. 23.
19. Nicholas Lash, Easter in the Ordinary, p. 275.
20. C. S. Lewis, A Grief Observed, London: Faber, 1962, pp. 52–53.